Preparing Masses with Children

15 Easy Steps

Robert W. Piercy, Jr.

LTP

LITURGY
TRAINING
PUBLICATIONS

Nihil Obstat
Very Reverend Daniel A. Smilanic, JCD
Vicar for Canonical Services
Archdiocese of Chicago
November 30, 2011

Imprimatur
Reverend Monsignor John F. Canary, STL, DMIN
Vicar General
Archdiocese of Chicago
November 30, 2011

The *Nihil Obstat* and *Imprimatur* are declarations that the material is free from doctrinal or moral error, and thus is granted permission to publish in accordance with c. 827. No legal responsibility is assumed by the grant of this permission. No implication is contained herein that those who have granted the *Nihil Obstat* and *Imprimatur* agree with the content, opinions, or statements expressed.

Author: Robert W. Piercy, Jr.

Special thanks to Nora Malone, Kate Cuddy, Deanna Keefe, Kimberly Krumviede, Denise La Giglia, Jo-Ann Metzdorff, Debbie Shimek, Judith Strohschein, and Colleen Quinn for their contributions to this book.

Library of Congress Control Number: 2011936399

16 15 14 13 12   1 2 3 4 5

ISBN 978-1-61671-049-1
PMC

This book is dedicated to
the children: my nieces and nephews,
my students, my friends, and all the
children who draw us closer to God.
Thank you for your awe
and wonder.

kelly seifert jaster

Contents

⟫ A Note for Teachers and Catechists

Now is your time! You and your group have been asked to prepare the Eucharistic liturgy. For some, this may be a simple and familiar process, and for others, this may be brand new, so the duties and responsibilities may seem overwhelming.

This book is here to help you, whether you're a math teacher planning your very first Mass or a school liturgist who has been doing this for 20 years. This book outlines a simple 15-step process, with one chapter dedicated to each step. These 15 simple steps will allow you to make sound judgments, adapt the preparation to fit your specific need, communicate effectively with others in your school and parish, and allow you to rest assured that you are doing the "right thing."

Over the years, our customers have come to us with many questions and concerns about planning liturgies with children. Again and again, we hear: "Do you have anything to help me plan the liturgy so that I don't get in trouble with the pastor/principal/liturgist?" As you begin to prepare the Mass, remember that liturgy is an expression of the community's praise and honor of the holy Eucharist. It is not about getting yourself "in trouble," or about being right or wrong. Sometimes, problems can arise between people involved in preparing liturgies with children because of your different outlooks and areas of expertise. Some parties involved may be very knowledgeable about the Church's liturgical norms and practices but not very good with children, while other parties involved know a lot about engaging children but are unaware of liturgical guidelines. This is a difficult situation for everyone involved. It is no fun arguing over things that you know are right, nor is it fun to feel as if you are being punished for not knowing things that no one ever explained to you. This book will give you the information that you need to work with others in your parish in a cooperative way with a mutual understanding of best liturgical practices for children.

This book will show you not just how to prepare liturgies, but how to prepare them with children. It is important that you include the children in the preparation of the celebration because, when you do, they see themselves in what happens at Mass. Then, Mass does not feel boring or confusing; it feels like the culmination of the things that they have been thinking and feeling. Would you send children onstage to perform in a school play without doing any preparation with them ahead of time? Of course not. Before a school play, teachers and students spend a great deal of time working together to explore the script, design costumes, plan sets, and practice songs. In the same way, you prepare the children for full participation in the Mass by involving them in the planning ahead of time.

This will be a different process than preparing your class for a play, though. It is a process that we call liturgical catechesis. The *Catechism of the Catholic Church* says, "Liturgical catechesis aims to initiate people into the mystery of Christ (It is 'mystagogy.') by proceeding from the visible to the invisible, from the sign to the thing signified, from the 'sacraments' to the 'mysteries'" (1075). Rather than teaching the children what you are doing in the Mass with explanations, practice, or lessons, liturgical catechesis requires that you teach the children by doing ritual: doing something over and over again until it becomes part of the fiber of their beings. It is not important that the children know what they are "supposed" to do; it is important that they're engaged in the experience of doing it. It is not important that the children understand everything that goes on; it is important that they see what happens in the liturgy and begin to wonder at it. There is a reason why we call it the Paschal *Mystery*—this is something that we will wonder at for our whole lives. Don't feel as if you need to be the one with all the answers, or that you need to prepare children for Mass as if you are preparing them to take a test. Leave space for the children to learn from the ritual itself and wonder at its meaning. This is part of the mystagogy that we'll examine later.

Preparing liturgies with children is challenging. It requires that you communicate with a variety of leaders in your church and parish. It requires that you remain humble and are ready to accept input from people with a wide variety of backgrounds and areas of expertise. It requires that you are willing to adapt the teacher/student relationship in order to leave space for liturgical catechesis. And, it requires a willingness to ask questions and ask for help when needed. As a teacher, you know firsthand that asking questions is an important part of growing in knowledge. Remember that there's no shame in asking for help when you need it.

So . . . let's take a deep breath and begin!

≫ A Note for Priests, Deacons, Liturgists, Musicians, Principals, and Directors of Faith Formation

Your role in the preparation of liturgies with children is to help and guide teachers and catechists as they develop children in their understanding not just of the liturgy, but of the preparation that goes into preparing a Eucharistic celebration.

As you work with teachers and catechists to prepare liturgies with children, acknowledge that you have varying areas of expertise. You are probably well versed in liturgical norms, and it can be frustrating to work with those who lack your understanding. Remember, though, that the teachers and catechists with whom you work are also experts in their own area of education and working with children. All of your areas of expertise need to come to the table in order to prepare a liturgically correct celebration that fully engages the children. All parties need to be ready to lower the stakes and treat one another with love, respect, and humility.

At the beginning of each school year, you may find it helpful to schedule a meeting with any teachers or catechists who may be involved in preparing liturgies in order to discuss the parameters that they are to follow as they prepare. Be ready to talk about the following areas:

- **Readings:** Which readings will you be using for your Masses? Will you be doing the weekday readings? Should the readings come from the Lectionary or from the *Lectionary for Masses with Children*? What resources can you recommend for help in interpreting the readings? If the teachers or catechists are ever concerned that a reading is too confusing or scary for children, who should they talk to?

- **Music:** Who will be selecting the music? If the teachers or catechists are to select the music, what resources are available for them to use? What guidelines do you have for the selection of music? Will any musicians, like a cantor, pianist, or organist, be available to help perform music?

- **Ministers:** Who will be finding ministers for various roles during the Mass, like greeters, readers, musicians, and those who bring the gifts forth? If the children will be performing these roles, what training or guidelines can you provide for them?

- **Who Does What:** Talk through the full course of the Mass, from start to finish, and identify who will be responsible for making decisions about, preparing, and performing each piece. Identify which aspects of the liturgy are negotiable and which aspects are not.

- **Schedule:** How far in advance will the pastoral team need a final outline of the liturgy? Who reviews this outline and approves it?

- **Questions / Concerns:** Identify a person who teachers and catechists can go to with their questions or concerns. You might also want to identify some resources, such as books or websites, that they can use as they are preparing.

- **Goals:** You may find it helpful to set a liturgical goal for the coming year, such as helping the students to better understand the Penitential Rite, or encouraging full participation in all sung responses. Communicate your goals to the teachers or catechists, and encourage them to think creatively about how these goals might be reached.

- **Logistics:** Make sure that teachers and catechists know how to access everything they will need for planning. Tell them which Lectionaries and hymnals they may use and where they can find them. If they will be responsible for liturgical environment, let them know what is available to them and when they may set up the church.

By settling these matters early in the year, you can make sure that everyone is on the same page and understands what needs to be done. This will help you move through the year with a common mission, rather than allowing different understandings or expectations to lead you into arguments. As you are working with teachers and catechists, remember that what you are doing is much bigger and more important than any one person's viewpoint. You are preparing the liturgies that will bring children to the table and keep them coming back throughout their lives.

The 15 Steps

1 Preparing to prepare. Begin by reviewing your parameters and planning ahead so that you are sure that you have the time and resources to pull this off. What exactly are you responsible for preparing? How will you integrate the children into your preparation? How will this fit into your teaching schedule?

2 Review the flow of the liturgy. Take time to reflect on the overall movement and significance of the parts of the Mass.

3 Select the readings. Review the readings that will be used.

4 Review the readings together. Introduce the readings to the children. Read a portion of the readings every day. Key in on words they remember.

5 Discuss and choose music. Once the readings are understood, begin to look for music using the key words that you heard in the readings.

6 Prepare students for their roles. Choose and prepare people to fill the different ministerial roles—readers, hospitality ministers, musicians, arrangers of liturgical environment, cantors, bearers of gifts, and, the most important role, the assembly.

7 Write the Prayer of the Faithful. Write intercessions as a class activity.

8 Work with the priest celebrant. Invite the priest celebrant to join the children for a dialogue on the readings.

9   Create the liturgical environment and integrate local needs and customs. Decide what, if anything, you will add to the liturgical environment, like banners, worship aids, or symbols. Be aware of any customs that may be celebrated in your community or in the families of some children in your group and consider how they might be incorporated into the liturgy.

10   Communicate with other faculty members and the catechetical team. Share some of what you've learned from preparing the liturgy with the children in your group with other teachers or catechists. Let them know what was most interesting to the children, or what activities or questions your group really responded to.

11   Rehearse. Help the children to get ready to perform any roles they may be taking during the liturgy.

12   Review the master checklist. On the day before the liturgy, make sure that everything is ready to go.

13   It's the day of the liturgy. Make sure that you're aware of everything that needs to be done, either by you, the sacristan, or another person, to prepare for the liturgy.

14   Be prepared to handle any situation during the liturgy. Stay calm and enjoy the liturgy, but be prepared to go to Plan B if someone misses a cue or cannot fulfill a role.

15   Mystagogy: What happened and what did you learn? Relive the experience of the liturgy with your group, and also do a personal reflection on what worked and what did not work.

Preparing to Prepare

⟳⟩ Be Aware of the Parameters

Have you ever had the experience of preparing a Mass, only to encounter irritation from your principal or pastor over your selection of readings or music? This kind of situation often arises when everyone is not on the same page. For this reason, it is very important that you understand the parameters of your situation ahead of time. If you are not clear on your principal, pastor, or director of faith formation's expectations, make sure that you ask questions until everything is clear.

The first thing you will need to know is which Mass you will be doing. Will you be using the Lectionary readings for the weekday when the Mass occurs? Will you be using the Lectionary readings for the coming Sunday? Make sure that you find this out ahead of time. You will also want to know which translation of the readings you will be using. Some schools and parishes use the *Lectionary for Masses with Children*, while others prefer to use the main Lectionary. If you need to use these books and do not know where they are kept, ask.

You also will want to know which parts of the Mass you need to prepare and facilitate. Will there be a reader in place to do the readings, or do you need to assign readers for them? Will someone else be selecting or performing the music, or will you be doing that? Do you need to assign children to serve as ushers / greeters or servers, or are there liturgical ministers assigned to this Mass? If you don't know the answers to these questions, keep asking until you are sure that you understand the extent of your responsibilities. You may want to keep a written record of the decisions that are made and provide copies to your pastor, principal, director of faith formation, and any other key players to ensure that everyone has the same understanding.

All About Masses with Children

In order to prepare the Mass with the children, you will need to be aware of the guidelines that govern all of the liturgies that we celebrate as a Church. A great starting point is the *General Instruction of the Roman Missal*. This document gives the overall norms for Catholic liturgy. There are also two documents, the Introduction to the *Lectionary for Masses with Children* and the *Directory for Masses with Children*, which speak specifically to liturgies with children. These two documents note the difference between Masses with adults where some children are also present, and Masses that are primarily attended by children.

In Masses where there is a mix of adults and children, care should be taken so that everyone can participate in the celebration of the liturgy together. Sometimes, this can be done by having the priest direct his introductory comments and homily to the children, but in such a way that adults can also benefit from it. Or, a parish might choose to do a separate Liturgy of the Word for children. In this case, the children leave the main assembly after the Introductory Rites and return before the beginning of the Liturgy of the Eucharist in order to celebrate the Liturgy of the Word, using the same basic format as the adults in the main assembly but with readings and a homily or reflection that are better suited to their needs and experiences. Many parishes with large numbers of small children do children's Liturgy of the Word at one or more of their Sunday Masses. If the Mass that you are preparing for will feature a combination of adults and children, then this is a good option for you.

Masses with children where few adults are present can be directed more clearly toward the children. The readings and music can be selected with the children in mind. The priest's comments and homily can be directed to the children. It is important to remember, though, that Masses adapted for children should help to prepare children for fuller participation in Masses with their families and the rest of their community. The Masses that you celebrate with children should not feel different from what is happening in your parish on Sunday. In fact, your Masses with the children are a great opportunity for you to prepare them for fuller participation on Sunday by introducing the prayers, gestures, and music of the Mass.

The *Directory for Masses with Children* and Introduction to the *Lectionary for Masses with Children* allow for some leeway in selecting readings, either for children's Liturgy of the Word or for a Mass where the majority of the assembly will be made up of children. These two documents allow the person preparing the liturgy to decide, with the help of the priest, which readings will be proclaimed. The Gospel reading must always be proclaimed. It is allowed, though, to shorten or even omit the other readings. There are two different sources that you can use for readings in Masses with mostly children present or children's Liturgy of the Word: the *Lectionary for Mass* and the *Lectionary for Masses with Children*. The *Lectionary for Mass* contains all of the readings that we use each day in our Masses as a Church. Sometimes, the readings in the *Lectionary for Mass* may be very well suited to the group of children that you work with, and sometimes you may need to shorten or omit some of the readings (so long as the Gospel is proclaimed). If your school or parish uses the *Lectionary for Masses with Children*, then the work of shortening or omitting readings has already been done for you. The *Lectionary for Masses with Children* was prepared specifically with children in mind. If you compare this to the main Lectionary, you will see that sometimes readings are shortened, omitted, or replaced with another, comparable reading.

For more information about the difference between the *Lectionary for Mass* and the *Lectionary for Masses with Children*, see page 19.

⟳ › Schedule When and How You Will Plan the Liturgy with Your Students

You will need to set aside six 30-minute periods in order to plan the liturgy with your students. You may choose to take time at the beginning or end of each day, or you may be able to think of ways in which planning the liturgy can coincide with some of the things that already are in your lesson plan.

The subsequent chapters of the book will give you detailed information on what will happen during each of these time periods. You will be covering the following content in six 30-minute sessions:

- **Session 1:** Listen to the Lectionary readings together and prepare a word map.

- **Session 2:** Discuss and select music.

- **Session 3:** If children will be taking any roles during the Mass, prepare them for their roles.

- **Session 4:** Write the Prayer of the Faithful.

- **Session 5:** Discuss the liturgical environment.

- **Session 6:** Rehearse and practice.

You will want to make sure that you have the following materials ahead of time in order to plan the liturgy:

- A Lectionary or Bible.

- A sheet of newsprint or section of the board that can remain untouched for several days to contain the word list.

- Hymnals.

 ## Trust the Process

Preparing liturgies with children can be scary because it requires that you let go of control and surrender yourself to ritual. As you prepare to work with the children, you'll need to enter into an attitude of wonder at the children's response to God, letting go of any pressure you feel to always be in control or have all of the answers.

In order to effectively plan liturgies with children, you need to trust that our liturgy is inherently appealing to children. The liturgy doesn't need to be dressed up or over-analyzed in order for children to become engaged by it. Our liturgy has aspects that appeal to every learning style built right into it. There are the visuals of liturgical colors, the auditory sounds of the readings and music, and the kinetic aspects of liturgical action. When given the opportunity to truly engage in the liturgy of our Church without being distracted by too many bells and whistles or over-directed by adults, children become wrapped up in the mystery and awe of the celebration of the Mass. As you prepare to work with the children, trust that this is true. Surrender any need you might have to provide explanation or any pressure you might feel to entertain the children. Believe that even the simplest aspects of the liturgy, when presented well, will not fail to grab the attention of every child.

You also will need to practice developing a different aspect of the teacher / student relationship as you begin to prepare liturgies with children. Rather than being the one with all of the answers, you need to take a role of awe and wonder along with the children. Your job is not to "teach" them the liturgy, but to provide them with an experience that will enable them to direct their own growth and development. Your role is to facilitate their relationship with God by providing them with a liturgical experience and allowing them to respond with wonder.

Life Story   Painting with Water

When I was teaching kindergarten, my class got invited to attend the Baptism of one of the children's baby brothers, so I felt I needed to teach them about Baptism. I thought, "Oh no, how am I going to do this?" I had an idea to get buckets of water and paint brushes, and took the kids outside to paint the brick walls of the school with the water. The children saw how the clear water went onto the dry bricks and made them darker and they said, "Look, the water changes it!" Of course, the poor pastor saw me out there with paint brushes and buckets and came screaming across the parking lot. "What are you doing?" he cried. "Just trust me," I said. "It's only water." The following Friday afternoon, we attended the Baptism as a group. When they put the baby over the font and the water was being poured over his forehead, one of the children said, "Look! The water changes him." "What do you mean?" I whispered. The child said, "Just like the water changes the bricks, the water changes him. He's now part of us." It was a profound moment for me. I knew that this child's realization was not a result of anything that I had done, but a result of the child's own inner workings and experience of God. We can't teach liturgy. Children grow in their understanding of liturgy out of their own experience of awe and wonder.

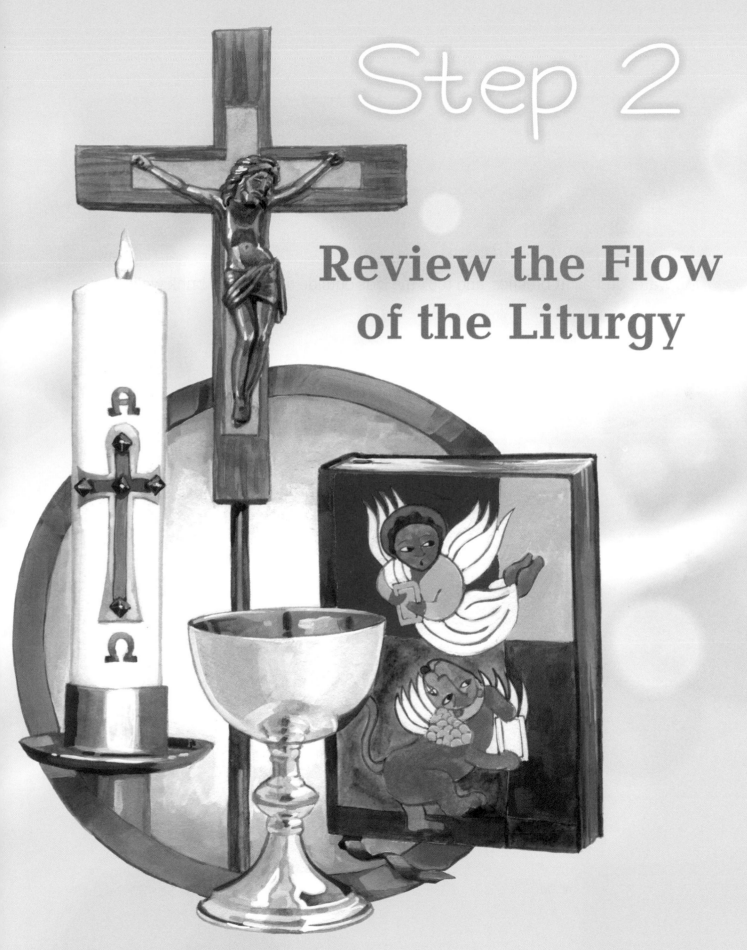

Step 2

Review the Flow of the Liturgy

The Parts of the Mass

When preparing liturgies with children, it is easy to focus only on those parts of the Mass in which your group will participate heavily, like the Liturgy of the Word, and forget about some of the other parts. Before preparing a liturgy with children, take time to review the parts of the Mass and their overall movement. You can see a summary of the parts of the Mass on this page.

The Parts of the Mass

Introductory Rites: The Introductory Rites unify the people and prepare them for the Liturgy of the Word and the Eucharist. We begin by processing in and singing an Entrance Song. The priest greets us, and we respond. Then, we pray the words of the Penitential Rite. We acknowledge our sins and receive a general absolution (this is not the same thing as a sacrament absolution). The priest asks that God will forgive us. After this, on Sundays or solemnities except during Advent and Lent, we sing the Gloria, an ancient hymn that glorifies God. Then, the priest says the Collect, which gathers (or "collects") the prayers of the people and expresses the character of the celebration.

Liturgy of the Word: After the Introductory Rites comes the Liturgy of the Word. At this time, we listen to the Word of God. The readings should be prepared prayerfully and carefully proclaimed from the ambo. There should be silence between them, so that the people hearing them can reflect on them meditatively. The readings that you hear will vary depending on the Mass that you are doing. If you are doing the weekday Mass, you will hear the First Reading (usually from the Old Testament, New Testament letters, or Acts of the Apostles), sing the psalm, prepare for the Gospel with a sung Gospel Acclamation ("Alleluia," except during Lent), and hear a reading from one of the four accounts of the Gospel. If you are doing the Sunday Mass or a Mass for a solemnity or feast day, you will hear the First Reading, sing the psalm, hear a Second Reading (usually from the letters of the New Testament), sing the Gospel Acclamation, and hear a reading from the Gospel. If you are using the *Lectionary for Masses with Children*, the readings may be different. Sometimes, if a reading is not considered suitable for children, it may be omitted from the Mass in the *Lectionary for Masses with Children*. For example, sometimes you may not have a Second Reading on a Sunday. The Gospel, the high point of the Liturgy of the Word, is always proclaimed.

After the readings, you will hear a homily or reflection. It is usually given by an ordained person, although in Masses with children, a reflection may be given by a lay person who has expertise in speaking to children. In Masses where children are predominately present, the homily might take the form of a conversation with the children, and may be more interactive than the typical homily. On Sundays, the homily or reflection is followed by a recitation of the Creed. In regular Masses we usually say the Nicene Creed, but many people prefer to use the Apostles' Creed in Masses with children. The Creed is followed by the Prayer of the Faithful or Universal Prayer, in which we bring forth our petitions for the needs of the Church, for the salvation of the world, and for specific needs in our community.

Liturgy of the Eucharist: In the Liturgy of the Eucharist, we remember the sacrifice that Christ made for us and receive Christ's Body and Blood. The Liturgy of the Eucharist begins with the Preparation of the Gifts. Members of the assembly bring the gifts of bread and wine and alms for the poor forward, often while the assembly sings a song. Then, the priest prays over the offerings and says the Eucharistic Prayer, which is considered the "center and summit" of the entire Eucharistic celebration. After the Eucharistic Prayer, we sing the Holy, Holy, Holy. Then the priest prays that the Holy Spirit will consecrate the gifts and reminds us of the institution of the Eucharist at the Last Supper. We affirm our belief by singing the Memorial Acclamation.

After the Memorial Acclamation, the Church offers the sacrificed Christ and we all offer ourselves. We pray intercessions, remembering that the Eucharist is celebrated in communion with the entire Church, heavenly and earthly. Then, we sing the "Amen."

The priest then leads the prayers of the Communion Rite. We all pray the Lord's Prayer and are invited to offer one another a sign of peace. After this, the priest breaks the host, signifying that we all receive from the one Christ, the Bread of Life. Then, the faithful process forward to receive communion while singing a hymn. After communion, we pray again.

> **Concluding Rites:** In the Concluding Rites, we are sent forth from Mass with Christ's mission to serve others. If there are any announcements that need to be made, they are made at this time. Then, the priest says a blessing over the people and sends them forth to do good works. We process from the church, sometimes singing a Closing Song.

The Liturgy is One Breath

Look over the parts of the Mass and recall liturgies with children that you have planned or attended in the past. What element would you identify as the high point, or what area is given the most attention in the liturgy? It can be easy to give primary focus to the parts of the Mass that you are most responsible for planning, like the Liturgy of the Word. While you are preparing these parts of the Mass, though, you cannot lose sight of their purpose and placement in the liturgy as a whole.

You must look at the entire liturgy as one breath, not as several different pieces or "acts." There is an ebb and flow to the liturgy. In the Opening Rites, we prepare ourselves for what is to come: the Liturgy of the Word and the Liturgy of the Eucharist. According to the *General Instruction of the Roman Missal* (GIRM), the Liturgy of the Word and Liturgy of the Eucharist should be "so closely interconnected that they form but one single act of worship" (28). These two parts build toward the Eucharistic Prayer, the "center and high point" of the Mass (GIRM, 78). From there, nourished by the Word of God and the Body and Blood of Christ, the Concluding Rites send us forth to serve as disciples.

As you are preparing the liturgy with children, remember why you are doing it. It isn't merely the fulfillment of a requirement. And it's not a school play where there is an audience. In fact, it is the assembly who does much of the work of liturgy. Make sure that this is in the front of your mind as you are preparing liturgies. What you are doing is teaching children the ritual language of the Church, preparing them for ongoing participation in the liturgy, and instilling the mission of discipleship within them. As you are planning the opening procession, remember that it is part of your preparation for the Liturgy of the Word and the Liturgy of the Eucharist. In light of this, an over-the-top opening procession does not really make sense, as it might distract from the true meaning of the Mass. If you spend a lot of time as a class preparing the readings for the Liturgy of the Word, make sure that you take time to talk to the children about how hearing these readings prepares them to receive the Body and Blood of Christ.

If you are preparing a weekday liturgy, keep in mind that participation in the weekday liturgy should be preparing the children for the Sunday liturgy, not standing in place of it. Given this, you might find it appropriate to use some of the same musical settings and hymns in your weekday liturgy as the parish uses at Mass on Sunday. If your parish will be using certain hymns throughout a certain season like Advent or Lent, for example, you can teach the children those hymns in preparation for your weekday Mass. Knowing the hymns will make the children more eager participants in Mass on Sunday. If the hymns that your parish is using are too hard for the children to learn, especially those children who cannot read, then you might consider just learning the refrains of the hymns.

As you and the children prepare for your liturgy, also keep in mind the mission to which we are called as a result of our participation in Mass. After the Mass is over, take time to talk to the children about what they experienced and reflect on what they might do to take what they heard in the Mass into their daily lives. You can also use the Mass as an opportunity to talk about the importance of community. If a child complains that the Mass is boring and doesn't want to participate, talk about how that child's presence is important to every other child in your group. We attend Mass Sunday after Sunday not just for ourselves, but for those around us. They rely on our prayers and company just as we rely on their prayers and company. This is the ministry of the assembly!

Don't Underestimate Ritual

When planning liturgies, people often want to add new elements because they think it makes the liturgy more fun or interesting. They say, "But if you don't add anything, it's boring!" Don't let yourself fall into this trap. Ritual is not boring. In fact, it's comforting for children (and adults, too). The Mass is a touchstone in our lives. We return week after week to the same place and perform the same actions. The Mass does not change, but that does not mean that it is boring. It is only boring when we fail to acknowledge how *we* have changed since we last participated in that ritual. Think of how you celebrate birthdays in your family. The celebration probably does not change too much from year to year, but it isn't boring because you are called to reflect on all of the ways in which *you* have changed since your last birthday.

At first glance, it may seem as if something that's been done before is not as exciting as something that is new, but consider the power of ritual in your own life. Your favorite meal isn't the one that you've never had; it's the one that you've had again and again. Your favorite jeans aren't the ones that are on the rack at the mall; they're the ones that are so full of holes that they can't leave the house any longer. The Mass can be like this for the children. It can become the favorite meal that never fails to satisfy.

Trust the ritual. Don't underestimate the power of singing the same songs that you already know and performing the same ritual that you have done before. Remember, too, that boredom can come when we don't understand the purpose and meaning of an event. Part of our work is to give the children time to contemplate the meaning behind our ritual.

Five Things to Avoid At All Costs

1. The Over-the-Top Entrance: We've all seen it happen—every single kid in the school parades in waving a banner and playing a musical instrument, to the point where a casual observer might not know whether you are preparing for Mass or practicing for the Macy's Thanksgiving Day parade. It is wonderful to get children involved in the opening procession of the Mass, but it is important that you keep it simple and dignified. For example, you might invite some children to process in carrying simple ribbon banners in the liturgical colors, or you might have some children process in carrying votive candles that can be placed somewhere at the front of the church. You can involve more children without making the procession overly long if you use all of the aisles in your space.

2. The Barely-Perceptible Liturgy of the Word: Be honest now—how many times have you heaved a sigh of relief after the Old Testament reading is completed out of pure gratitude that the child proclaiming it made it all the way to the end? Reading scripture aloud is difficult for adults, so it should come as no surprise that a child who has just mastered *The Cat in the Hat* might have some trouble tackling the strange names of people and places and unusual turns of phrase that are in many scripture readings. While it may seem vital to give every child a "part," remember that being a member of the assembly is an important "part," too. The assembly deserves to hear the readings proclaimed in a prayerful, meditative way. If you are working with younger children to prepare the liturgy, consider looking outside of your group for appropriate readers. Perhaps you might invite a parent or older sibling to serve as a reader. Maybe you could ask the school librarian, or another adult who often reads stories to the children. Then, you might select a few children who can help the readers.

A child can come forward with the reader when the time comes and proclaim, "A reading from the book of . . . ." The child can stand next to the adult or older child while he or she reads, and then come forth again to proclaim, "The word of the Lord."

3. The Presentation of Everything but the Kitchen Sink: The Presentation of the Gifts can, at school Masses, sometimes get a bit out of control. When all is said and done, everything that isn't nailed down winds up heaped on top of the altar. While it is wonderful to have classroom objects blessed, this is not the time for that. The things that we bring to the altar during the Preparation of the Gifts are not things that we expect to get back. When we send money to the altar during the Sunday Mass, we don't expect to come up and take back blessed dollar bills when the Mass is over. We are giving that money for the good of someone else, just as Jesus gave his life for the good of all of us. The things that we bring forward represent sacrifice of the self on behalf of others: the Eucharistic species of bread and wine represent Christ's sacrifice for us, and the money that we give represents our sacrifice for the Church, the Body of Christ. Make this clear to the children by keeping it simple and only bringing forth those things that you are giving of yourselves for someone else. If you are doing a food drive, for example, then it is appropriate to bring the cans of food forward and place them at the altar.

4. Symbol Overload: Sometimes, in an attempt to make Masses with children more engaging, we can fall into the trap of symbol overload. Everywhere you look, there's a different symbol: light, water, sand, lilies, lions, tigers, bears, oh my! When planning your liturgy, remember the value of austerity. When you are first teaching someone to play the piano, you start with a simple scale, not the showiest concerto. In the same way, when you are introducing children to the liturgy, it is important to start simple. As you and the children work through the readings, notice if there is one pervasive symbol and focus on that. You can also just focus on the colors and symbols of the time of the liturgical year. Remember that you are using symbols to enhance, not distract from, the liturgy. Avoid obvious symbols and allow the children to wonder at what they see in the church. Remember, you are creating liturgy that children will grow into, not out of.

5: The Theme That Just Won't Quit: Sometimes, in an effort to make the Mass more appealing to children, a theme like "friendship" or "peace" is applied to it . . . and suddenly, the theme takes over—you are reading friendship readings, singing friendship songs, saying friendship prayers, and leave the Mass unable to think of anything but the friendship theme! When preparing your liturgy, remember that the Mass already has a "theme"—the Paschal Mystery, the heart of our faith: Christ died for us, rose from the dead, and will come again. You don't need to add anything to the Mass to give it meaning. It has a meaning greater than anything we could ever apply to it. Allow the rhythm of the liturgy and liturgical year to take over, and allow yourself to relax and wonder at the children's response.

Step 3
Select the Readings

› # Know Which Mass You Are Doing

The first step in selecting the readings is knowing what is required of you. In Step 1, you should have reviewed the parameters and identified which readings you will be using: those from the Sunday Mass or those from the weekday Mass. If you aren't sure which day of the liturgical year it will be, you can find this out by referring to a missalette, liturgical calendar, or reading reference. You can also ask your pastor or liturgist for guidance.

A Brief Primer on the Liturgical Year

Just as the secular world organizes its days, holidays, and seasons using a calendar, the Church uses the liturgical calendar to count time, celebrate special days, and encourage our spiritual growth. Schools already have a secular calendar full of holidays, vacations, academic themes, birthdays, natural seasons, and so on, and it can be tempting to allow your liturgies to reflect these things rather than keep them focused on what is happening on the liturgical calendar. Don't let yourself fall victim to this temptation. The liturgical year is rich with colors, symbols, stories, rituals, and mysteries of our faith that never stop drawing us to new, deeper realizations and questions. Trust in the power of the liturgy, and trust in the power of the liturgical year.

Balancing the liturgical year and the secular year does not mean that you have to force your students' attention away from the secular milestones in their lives. Find ways to incorporate those things into your liturgies while still giving the liturgical season primary focus.

The liturgical year is broken out into the following periods:

Advent (begins four Sundays before Christmas and ends after midafternoon prayer on Christmas Eve).

We call the days and nights before Christmas Advent, which means "coming." The Church reads and sings about God's promises. We tell stories of many holy people: Mary and John the Baptist, Nicholas and Lucy. We strive for the time when God's love will be seen in all of us, when peace will be seen in people's acts of justice and love for each other. But primarily, we wait. We wait in joyful hope for the coming of our Savior, Jesus

Christ, when all will be one, and the kingdom of God will flourish. The Son of God already came to us, born in the city of David. This is what we celebrate at Christmas, and in Advent, we ready ourselves and our hearts for this birth. But, we also wait for his coming again. We wait for his light to completely extinguish our darkness.

Christmas Time (begins with Evening Prayer on Christmas Eve and ends after evening prayer on the Feast of the Baptism of the Lord).

On December 25, we proclaim, "Today is born our Savior, Christ the Lord." And so begins the celebration of the Lord's birth, of God becoming man. God loved us so much that he gave his only Son to be one with us, to end all pain, and to bring us eternal light. And so we celebrate the gift of his love. We fill the long darkness with beautiful lights. We sing carols and eat delicious food. Around the festive trees, we give one another gifts because God has given such good gifts to us, and we open our homes to guests because God has opened heaven to us.

Lent (begins on Ash Wednesday and ends before the celebration of the evening Mass of the Lord's Supper on Holy Thursday).

The 40 days of Lent are not literally 40, but the number evokes all other uses of "40" in the scriptures. For 40 days, Jesus fasted and prepared to proclaim the Good News. Long before Jesus, Moses and Elijah had their 40-day fasts. It rained on the earth and on Noah's ark for 40 days, and the earth had a new beginning. And for 40 years the people of Israel wandered in the wilderness toward the Promised Land. In the Bible, the number 40 means that something important is taking place.

We enter Lent with ashes on our heads, and during the remaining days we fast in various ways, perhaps by eating less food and foregoing treats. We give alms, which means that we find ways to share what we have: our time and our goods. In these ways, we remember our Baptism and so try to grow more deeply in the Christian life.

The Sacred Paschal Triduum (begins on Holy Thursday with the evening Mass of the Lord's Supper and ends after Evening Prayer on Easter Sunday).

Paschal Triduum means the "Three Days." For the Jewish people, Passover celebrates the great event when God delivered the people of

Israel from slavery. The followers of Jesus proclaim that in the life, Passion, Death, and Resurrection of Jesus, God has freed and saved us.

When Lent ends, we stand at the heart of the liturgical year. On the night of Holy Saturday and Easter Sunday we keep the Easter Vigil. We gather to light a great fire and a towering candle, to listen to our most treasured scriptures, and to sing psalms and other songs. Then, we gather around the waters of the font as those who have been preparing for new life in Christ receive the sacraments of initiation. The newly baptized are then anointed with a fragrant oil called chrism; and, at last, with these newly baptized, who are now called neophytes, we celebrate the Eucharist.

We prepare for this Vigil by celebrating the institution of the Holy Eucharist on Holy Thursday and by commemorating the Lord's Passion by venerating the cross on Good Friday. We also prepare by keeping the Paschal fast, the special fast of Good Friday and Holy Saturday. The Church fasts—from food, entertainment, chatter, and work—so we have time to ponder deeply the Death and Resurrection of the Lord, the mystery of faith that we will celebrate in our Vigil.

Easter Time (begins on Easter Sunday and ends after Evening Prayer on Pentecost Sunday).

Easter is 50 days. Easter Sunday is to the year what Sunday is to the week. We live as if God's kingdom has already come—because it has. We put aside our fasting for feasting and celebration. We bless ourselves with baptismal water to remind us of our share in Jesus' Passion, Death, and Resurrection. "Alleluia" is our song because we delight to praise the Lord. The stories we read from scripture are of Thomas's and Mary Magdalene's encounters with the risen Lord, of meals with Jesus, of the Good Shepherd, and of the outpouring of the Holy Spirit.

Ordinary Time (lasts from evening prayer on the Feast of the Baptism of the Lord until Ash Wednesday, and then again from after evening prayer on Pentecost Sunday until evening prayer of the First Sunday of Advent).

For a few weeks in January and February, and then all through the summer and fall, the Church is in Ordinary Time. Ordinary comes from the word *ordinal*, and means "counted." In other words, each of the weeks has a number (for example, the Third Sunday in Ordinary Time).

Ordinary Time is full of solemnities, feasts, and memorials of the Lord and the saints. In its last weeks, we keep All Saints Day on November 1, and All Souls Day on November 2. The whole month of November becomes a time to rejoice in the communion of saints and to remember that our true home is in the heavenly Jerusalem.

Know Which Lectionary You Are Using

You have two options of Lectionaries: the *Lectionary for Mass* or the *Lectionary for Masses with Children.*

1. The Lectionary for Mass: The *Lectionary for Mass* contains all of the readings used in all Roman Catholic Churches. It has materials for all of the Masses that will be celebrated throughout the year, including special Masses for various occasions. There are six parts of the *Lectionary for Mass:* the Proper of Seasons, which is divided into Sunday Readings and Weekday Readings; the Proper of the Saints, which is arranged by calendar date from January through December; Commons; Ritual Masses; Masses for Various Occasions; and Votive Masses. You probably will mostly be dealing with the first section: the Proper of Seasons. On occasions when a saint's feast is celebrated instead of the regular Mass of the day, you will use readings from the Proper of Saints or the Commons. You will want to confer with a liturgical calendar and your pastor or liturgist in order to know which readings you will be using.

Within the Proper of Seasons, Sunday readings are separated from weekday readings. The Sunday readings are arranged in a three-year cycle. The three years are called Year A, Year B, and Year C. Each cycle begins with the First Sunday of Advent (the first Sunday of the liturgical year) and concludes with the Solemnity of Our Lord Jesus Christ, King of the Universe (the last Sunday of the liturgical year, and the Sunday right before Advent begins). You can find out which cycle you currently are in by asking your pastor or liturgist. For each Sunday there are three readings—the First Reading, the Second Reading, and the Gospel—and a Responsorial Psalm that is recited or sung (it is better to sing) between the first two readings. The readings are not in the Lectionary in chronological order. The readings for Advent, Christmas, Lent, and Easter come first, and the readings for Ordinary Time are after them.

The weekday readings are structured somewhat differently. There are only two readings on weekdays: the First Reading, and the Gospel. A responsorial psalm is recited or sung (again, it is best practice to sing) between the First Reading and the Gospel. The weekday readings in the Lectionary also are arranged with Advent, Christmas, Lent, and Easter first, and the readings for Ordinary Time coming behind. The weekday readings are not divided into the three Years A, B, and C like the Sunday readings are. Instead, the weekday readings for the seasons of Advent, Christmas, Lent, and Easter are the same every year. During Ordinary Time, the Gospel for the weekday readings is the same every year, and the choice of First Reading is given in a two-year cycle. The two years are referred to as Year I and Year II. We hear the First Readings from Year I in odd-numbered years, and the First Readings from Year II in even-numbered years.

The Proper of Saints contains Masses assigned to the feast days and memorials of saints. Sometimes, you might find that only one reading is given for a Mass in the Proper of Saints. When this happens, another reading is selected from the Commons. You will want to ask for the guidance of your pastor or parish liturgist in these situations.

2. The Lectionary for Masses with Children: The *Lectionary for Masses with Children* is intended for Masses where there are large numbers of preadolescent children present, or for children's Liturgy of the Word. This doesn't mean that the *Lectionary for Masses with Children* should be used in any setting where there are children. According to the Introduction of the *Lectionary for Masses with Children,* the *Lectionary for Mass* should always "take precedence over the *Lectionary for Masses with Children* in the main assembly of the faithful" (13). In your school or religious education program's liturgies with children, though, you may find that the readings in the *Lectionary for Masses with Children* are more appropriate.

The *Lectionary for Masses with Children* was written in order to adapt what is in the *Lectionary for Mass* to make it better suited to the "needs and capacities" of children (*Lectionary for Masses with Children,* Introduction, 11). You will find that the wording of the readings in the *Lectionary for Masses with Children* differ from the readings in the *Lectionary for Mass.* The *Lectionary for Masses with Children* uses the Contemporary English Version of the Bible instead of the New American Bible, which is what the *Lectionary for Mass* uses. Sometimes, the readings in the *Lectionary for Masses with Children* are altered in order to make them more understandable for younger listeners.

When using the *Lectionary for Masses with Children,* you may find that the selection of readings can also differ from what appears in the *Lectionary for Mass.* The *Lectionary for Masses with Children* always has the same Gospel selection as the *Lectionary for Mass,* but sometimes it is a shortened version. The First and Second Readings usually are the same as they are in the *Lectionary for Mass,* but not always. In cases where the First or Second Reading is considered too obscure, abstract, or confusing for children, it may be eliminated or replaced with another reading. It also may be omitted occasionally.

The *Lectionary for Masses with Children* is also organized somewhat differently than the *Lectionary for Mass*. The Sunday readings in the *Lectionary for Masses with Children* are organized just as they are in the *Lectionary for Mass*, divided into Years A, B, and C. There are not, however, as many delineated sets of weekday readings in the *Lectionary for Masses with Children* as there are in the *Lectionary for Mass*. There are 36 sets of readings in the *Lectionary for Masses with Children* that can be used throughout Ordinary Time. They are not divided into Years I and II as they are in the *Lectionary for Mass*. These selections of readings represent all four accounts of the Gospel and correspond with the themes and images in the readings for the coming Sunday and the liturgical time as a whole. It is also important to note that there are no readings in the *Lectionary for Masses with Children* for the three days of the Paschal Triduum: Holy Thursday, Good Friday, and the Easter Vigil on Holy Saturday. The liturgies for these days speak for themselves, and should require no adaptation for children.

Where can I get a copy of the *Lectionary for Masses with Children?*

At the time of printing, texts of the *Directory for Masses with Children* and the *Lectionary for Masses with Children* are awaiting confirmation from the Vatican. Because the texts are being revised, publishers cannot produce new copies of the *Lectionary for Masses with Children*, and so the book is out of print. Even though the book is out of print, it is still approved for use in liturgies with children until the time when the revised version is available. If your parish or school does not have a copy, you might be able to find one at a used bookstore. Websites that sell used books, such as www.amazon.com, www.ebay.com, and www.alibris.com, may also have copies available for sale.

Finding the Lectionary Readings

In order to locate the readings for a certain day in the *Lectionary for Mass* or *Lectionary for Masses with Children,* you will need to know whether you are looking for a weekday or Sunday reading, what liturgical time or season you are in, and what cycle you are in (A, B, or C for Sunday readings, I or II for weekday readings in the *Lectionary for Mass*). Once you know those things, finding the reading is not too difficult. Remember that the seasons of Advent, Christmas, Lent, and Easter come ahead of Ordinary Time.

If you have a missalette, liturgical calendar, or another reference, you can just refer to that to find out which Lectionary readings you need to prepare. Your reference may give you a Lectionary number along with the date. Each set of Lectionary readings for a given day has a Lectionary number attached to it. Usually, the Lectionary number appears at the top of the page of readings. The Lectionary numbers in the *Lectionary for Mass* and the Lectionary numbers in the *Lectionary for Masses with Children* are not the same.

Selecting the Readings Yourself

Sometimes, in a desire to implement a certain theme or apply a certain idea to a liturgy, teachers or catechists select readings from the Bible on their own. This is not advisable. The readings in the Lectionary have been selected carefully to correspond with the flow of the liturgical year and to build upon one another to tell the story of salvation. There is no need to break away from this. The only time you should choose readings on your own is on weekdays during Ordinary Time when using the *Lectionary for Masses with Children.* Then, just pick from the selections given in the *Lectionary for Masses with Children.*

If you are reviewing the readings and come across one that you think will be too confusing or difficult for the children, find out who you need to consult in order to work out a solution. *The Directory for Masses with Children* grants the permission to omit a reading so long as it is not the Gospel reading, replace a reading with another reading appropriate to that time of the liturgical year, or omit some verses so long as the primary meaning of the text is preserved. There is no need to suffer through a reading that children may misunderstand. Work with the priest celebrant or liturgist to come up with a viable solution. In Masses with children, quality of readings is more important than quantity. It could be that the short form of the Gospel, proclaimed very well, is much more effective for the children with whom you work than rattling off three readings that they do not understand.

Review the Readings on Your Own

Before discussing the readings with the children, you will want to read them and reflect on them yourself. Look at the list of questions you will be asking the children, and prepare to discuss them together (see the box titled, "Talking about Lectionary Readings with Children").

Begin by going through the readings once, straight through. Note any words or concepts that are confusing to you or that might be confusing for the children. You may want to use a Catholic Study Bible for more information about the context of the readings so that you can share what you learn with the children. Often some concepts and images in scripture stories are rooted in the familiar objects and situations of life in biblical times, so a little bit of historical context can really help in understanding the readings. Take note of any words that the children may not know, and find definitions for them that you think the children will understand. When you do this, select two or three words that you will define for the children before hearing the readings. You will only want to explain words that are certain to confuse and that are critical to the overall understanding of the reading. Avoid defining too many terms—you don't want to miss out on an opportunity for the children to discover the meanings of new words on their own from context clues.

As you prepare to discuss the readings with the children, remember that, while your ability to provide them with definitions of difficult words and historical context is important, you are going to be listening and discussing the readings *together*. Your role as a teacher is to do everything you can to support their experience of listening and responding, not to be the one with all of the answers. Be ready to welcome the children's ideas and interpretations with openness, affirming their experience of the Word of God. You, too, will hear new things!

Talking about Lectionary Readings with Children

1. Give a brief context for the reading. Tell the children what book of the Bible the reading comes from, who they will be hearing about in the reading, and what situation is being addressed. If the setting is important (for example, the Jordan River), you may want to share a picture of it.

2. Define some words (no more than three) that may be unfamiliar to the children.

3. Read the reading aloud. You might read it yourself, or if the children in your group are old enough to read well, select a few children to read, perhaps assigning each a verse or paragraph.

4. Allow a few moments of silence after reading. Then ask the children: "What did you hear that really stood out to you? What did it mean to you? What part of this reading do you really want to remember?"

5. Record any words, phrases, or themes that stood out to the children on your word chart.

Life Story Get Ready!

My sister is a second grade teacher at a Catholic school in the Chicago suburbs. One evening, two days before Thanksgiving, I got a panicked call from her. Her second graders had prepared a Mass for the following day, and she had just found out that no priest celebrant was available. After I calmed her down, I pointed out that, with some changes, she could still do a prayer service that would be led by a lay presider. We walked through each step of the liturgy, making plans for what would need to be reworked. At the end of our phone call, she said, "So wait, who is this presider you keep mentioning?" I said, "It's you!" and then hung up the phone before she could argue! I'm sure that she was worried about taking on such a big role at the last minute, but I knew that she already knew the readings and liturgy inside out, and that her preparation would give her the confidence she needed to lead her school in prayer.

Preparation can be easy to put off or forego in the face of other things that need your attention, but the time that you spend reflecting on the flow of the liturgy and praying with the readings is the basis for all of the work that your class will be doing. It enables you to remain focused on the big picture and helps you to convey the spirit of the liturgy to others.

Step 4

Review the Readings Together

WATER
LIGHT
HOLY SPIRIT
MERCY
FORGIVENESS

Prepare Your Space

Even though the work that you do in your classroom is just preparation for the liturgy at Mass, it is still important that you model reverence for the Word of God in whatever way you can. If possible, proclaim the readings from a Lectionary or Bible rather than from a sheet of paper. Handle the book reverently and encourage the children to do the same. If you are using a piece of paper, you may want to consider covering a binder with a piece of white cloth and painting a gold cross on the front of it, to create a dignified holder for your sheets of paper.

Consider setting up an area in your classroom that will only be used for preparing the liturgy. Find a space in your classroom where the children can sit on the floor. Set up a prayer table in this space. You can use a small end table or a sturdy cardboard box for this purpose. Cover your table with a cloth that corresponds with the liturgical color of the time or season you are in (violet for Lent and Advent, white for Christmas and Easter, and green for Ordinary Time). On top of the cloth, place a candle (you can use a LED candle if real candles are not allowed in your classroom), a crucifix, an icon of Christ or a Mary statue if you like, and your Lectionary or Bible. Nearby, you will also want to have an area where you can create your word chart. This can be a section of the board that can be left filled for a while, a sheet of chart paper, or a piece of butcher paper taped to the wall.

When it is time to work on preparing the liturgy, gather the children around you on the floor in this space. Light the candle and open with a simple prayer, such as the Sign of the Cross or the Glory Be. At the end of your time preparing the liturgy together, close with a simple prayer and then extinguish the candle. This will help the children to see that the work you do to prepare the liturgy is different from the work you do to prepare for other things like tests or projects. Practicing these small rituals in your classroom prepares the children to engage in the ritual of the Mass.

Talking about Scripture with Children in Five Steps

Use the following five steps to talk about the readings with the children. You will want to repeat these five steps for each of the readings that you will be discussing, if possible. Depending on your time, you may want to do this all on one day, or you may choose to break the readings up across a few days.

Step 1: Give a brief context for the reading. Begin by telling the children something about the reading they will be hearing. Tell them what book of the Bible it is from, and a little bit about that book. Tell them a bit about any people or places they'll hear about, and give them a short synopsis of what will happen. For example, you might say, "In this reading from the Book of the prophet Isaiah, we hear God's words of comfort to the people of Israel after they were taken to exile in Babylon," or "In this reading from the Gospel according to Luke, we hear about Jesus' cousin John the Baptist, who prepared everyone for Jesus by telling them that they needed to change their evil ways and get ready."

Step 2: Explain some words (no more than three) that may be unfamiliar to the children. Don't define every word in the reading, but do define any words or concepts that might prove to be real stumbling blocks. If the reading mentions a leper, for example, you might want to explain what leprosy is before doing the reading. If the reading consistently features the word *repent*, you might want to talk to the children about how they understand that word before moving forward.

Step 3: Read the reading aloud. Depending on the reading ability of the children, you may want to either read the reading aloud yourself, or allow one or more of the children to proclaim the reading. If you would like to get a few children involved in proclaiming the reading, decide ahead of time how you will divide it (by verse, by paragraph). No matter who proclaims the reading, make sure that it is proclaimed slowly and reverently. If a child is proclaiming the reading, he or she should stand in front of the rest of the children, holding the Bible or Lectionary.

Step 4: Allow a few moments of silence, then reflect with questions. When the reading is finished, allow a few moments of silence. Then, talk to the children about what they heard in the reading. Try to avoid correcting the children or negating anything that they say. Redirect them where necessary, but focus on affirming their experience of the Word of God. You will want to let the conversation develop organically, but you may want to use some of the following questions as conversation starters:

 What did you hear that really stood out to you? What did it mean to you?

🌀 Who was speaking in this reading? What did that speaker say?

🌀 What do we learn about God in this reading?

🌀 What words were used in this reading?

🌀 What part of this reading do you most want to remember? Why?

Step 5: Record any words, phrases, or themes that stood out to the children on your word chart. As you are talking through each reading, keep track of words and ideas that stand out to the children by writing them down on a word chart. The word chart can be on a section of the board that can be left alone for a while, a sheet of chart paper, or a sheet of butcher paper taped to the wall. As you talk through the readings, put all of the words that the children notice onto the same word chart. Circle or underline words that seem to be coming up again and again. For example, if the children mention that they hear the word *light* in the First Reading and then it comes up again in the psalm, underline it to make that clear. You will be using this word chart for additional planning in steps to come, so make sure that you keep it intact. You may want to consider doing a video recording of your work with the children, in case the priest celebrant cannot come to meet with your group but is interested in seeing your work. Many digital cameras and cell phones have the ability to make videos that can easily be e-mailed from one person to another.

Processing Scripture through Artistic Expression

Depending on time and the ages and learning styles present in your group, you may wish to suggest different ways in which the children might express their feelings about the readings. Consider the following activities, or design some of your own:

• What physical movements do these words or stories suggest to the young people? How might they act out phrases, verses, or ideas with their bodies without using words (like in charades)?

• Allow the young people to use paint, drawing materials, clay, paper, or other craft materials to visually represent their favorite verse, story, or idea from the readings.

• If something in one of the scripture stories that you hear is commonly represented in fine art (such as the Immaculate Conception, Jesus and the Apostles, angels), bring in some images to show to the young people, and talk about how they relate to the readings.

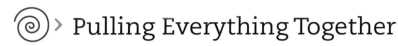 Pulling Everything Together

Once you are finished with your word chart, take time to look at it as a group. Notice any words or phrases that came up often, or that seem similar to one another. Notice if there are any words or phrases that seem to contradict one another, like *dark* and *light,* or *hope* and *sadness*. Also, take time to talk about the liturgical time or season that you are in. How do the words on your word chart support the symbols and mood of the time of the liturgical year? Leave your word chart in place—you will be using it again.

Step 5
Discuss and Choose Music

Know the Parameters

Before beginning to plan music, make sure that you understand the parameters that already are in place. Ask yourself the following questions and think about the things that your school usually does at Mass:

Are there teachers, staff members, or students who typically cantor and provide accompaniment? • Does the parish music director ever become involved with school Masses?

Who needs to review and approve the list of music the class chooses?

Is there any "must use" music? • Do you typically use certain settings for the Mass acclamations (like the Alleluia and Holy, Holy, Holy), for example? • Which pieces are already set, and which pieces should your class be choosing?

What hymnals or songbooks does your school usually use?

Prepare to Discuss Music

Before you discuss music with the children in your group, make sure that you know how many songs you will be choosing, and for what parts of the Mass. Use the "Music in the Mass" list to identify which parts of the Mass will need music chosen, and which parts already have music in place.

Some of the sung parts of the Mass are words straight from the Order of Mass. For the most part, the words of these parts do not change week to week (these parts are in italics in the "Music in the Mass" list). Ordinarily, schools and parishes have settings of the Mass that they use on a regular basis. The Mass setting that you use will most likely cover music for a large part of the Mass, including the Gloria; Gospel Acclamation; Holy, Holy, Holy; Memorial Acclamation; Amen; and Lamb of God. If it is up to you to pick a Mass setting, try to identify something with which the children are familiar so that they can participate easily. Generally, it is good practice to use the Mass setting that is used by the parish on Sundays. This way, the children grow familiar with the music they will be singing at Mass. If you don't use the one that the parish uses on Sunday, decide on one setting to use as a school and commit to it for the whole year.

For the Responsorial Psalm, you can pick a musical setting, but you do not pick the psalm itself. The psalm is one of the readings in the Lectionary and is already set for you. When thinking about the psalm, remember that it is part of scripture, just like the other readings. It should be led from the ambo, or if that is not possible, the psalm may be proclaimed from "another suitable place" (GIRM, 61). It should be proclaimed well, just as the other readings should be proclaimed well. While people sometimes recite the psalm, it is best practice to sing it. You may have a strong cantor among the children in your group who can understand the meaning of the psalm's words and express them through volume, phrasing, and voice quality. If, however, you do not have a child who is a very strong singer within your group, you might try something else. You can see if there is an experienced cantor who can join you, perhaps one of your staff members or one of the children's parents. You can also select three or four children who can sing the psalm together, standing around the ambo. This is not ideal, but it does reduce the pressure of having a single student sing alone in front of the entire school. You might also invite a student cantor to chant the words of the psalm on a single note, and have the assembly respond by chanting the response on that same note.

There are several places in the Mass where we typically sing a familiar hymn. Selection of these hymns is not dictated by the Order of Mass or the Lectionary. These hymns are to be selected to "correspond with the spirit of the liturgical action" and to "foster the participation of all the faithful" (GIRM, 41). Ordinarily, these are the songs that you and your group will be picking. Usually, we sing hymns in the following places: Entrance Song, Preparation of the Gifts, Communion Song, Closing Song. For these parts, pick hymns that suit the liturgical time or season and scripture. Keep the logistics of what is happening in mind, as well. The entrance song, for example, should be something that suits what you have planned for a procession. The communion song should reflect what is happening—reception of the Body and Blood of Christ—and should have a refrain that is easy to remember so that people can continue to sing as they walk forth to receive communion.

Before meeting with the children, create a large chart indicating each part of the Mass for which you are choosing music. Leave space so that you can write the name of the song that you select next to each part as you are working.

Music in the Mass

The italicized items are part of the Order of Mass. The selection of one Mass setting will cover all of these items. Generally, it is best if you use the Mass setting that is ordinarily used by your parish on Sundays.

- Entrance Song
- *Gloria* (only if the Mass will be on a Sunday, solemnity, feast, or other celebration)
- Responsorial Psalm (sometimes, this is proclaimed, but best practice is to sing)
- *Gospel Acclamation*
- Preparation of the Gifts
- *Holy, Holy, Holy*
- Memorial Acclamation
- *Amen*
- *Lamb of God*
- Communion Song
- Closing Song

⟳ › Discuss Music with Your Group

In order to discuss music selections with your group, you will need to have your word chart (created in Step 4), a chart of music that needs to be selected, a copy of your parish hymnal for every child in your group, and, if possible, recordings of some possible songs.

Explain that you are selecting songs that will set the tone for the whole Mass, so it is important to choose songs that fit with the liturgical time or season and the scripture that will be proclaimed. The children should also keep in mind who will be singing the songs that they pick. Selecting an unfamiliar song with lots of words might prove difficult for younger children who are not yet strong readers, for example.

Distribute hymnals, and show the children a little bit about how they are used. Point out that, even though the books seem really big and long, there are ways to find the songs that you need. Show them the sections of seasonal hymns and the sections for set Mass parts. Show them how the indexes in the back can be used to locate songs with certain words or themes.

Next, refer to your word chart. Read through it again as a group. Talk about the words that seem most important. Divide the children into small groups, and assign each group a word or two. Have them go through the hymnals, looking for hymns that contain these words. Go around from group to group as they work, guiding them in their selections.

Once each group has identified some hymns, have them report back to the big group. Assess which songs are the best by thinking about their relation to the season and readings, how well the children know them, and where they might be used in the Mass. Once song selections are finalized, list them on your chart. Tell the children that you will be proposing these songs to the others on your pastoral team. Write down hymns that were suggested but not selected in case you need to change some of the songs. If you need to have your songs approved by the liturgist or music minister, bring your list to that person.

Selecting and Preparing Ministers

Once the music has been approved, consider who will take roles in leading the music. Again, keep your parameters in mind. At your school, are there adults who typically accompany and sing at Masses? Or do students traditionally take these roles? If adults typically take these roles, make sure they know what songs they will be leading. If children typically take these roles, consider the musicians in your group. Do you have any strong, confident singers? Are there any musicians in your group? Without sacrificing the integrity of the music, identify and prepare some music leaders. If you have a large number of musicians in your group, you might select different musicians for each song. Keep in mind that a full experience of worship is much more important than having a "part" in the Mass. If anxiety over leading music in front of others is going to cloud a child's experience of the Mass, then see if you can identify someone else, such as a parent or staff member, to take over the role of music leader.

Worship Aids

You may choose to make worship aids that include, among other things, references to your music selections. If you simply list information about the song, like the title, composer, and page in the hymnal, then you don't need to worry about copyrights. If you include the music of songs, or even just the text of lyrics of songs, though, then it is your responsibility to model good citizenship by ensuring that you have obtained the appropriate permissions.

In most cases, obtaining permission to reprint hymns will be relatively easy. Many parishes and schools have license agreements with the three major

Catholic music publishers: GIA, Oregon Catholic Press (OCP), and World Library Publications (WLP). If this is the case, you can just check with your parish or school liturgist or music minister to find out what copyright information and license number needs to appear beneath each of the songs. If you do not have a license or have selected music from a publisher with which you do not have an agreement, then you will need to go straight to the publisher to obtain permission.

Opening and Closing Processions

If your school or parish traditionally involves the children in opening or closing processions, plan these once you have selected music. You can involve several children in the procession by adding roles for children to carry banners or candles.

Be careful that you don't turn the procession into a Broadway production. Any decorations that the children carry should be simple and dignified. It is easy to make banners in liturgical colors by fastening two dowel rods into a "T" shape with glue or a small nail and then tying ribbons or strips of fabric in the appropriate colors (shades of green for Ordinary Time, violet and rose pink for Advent and Lent, white and gold for Easter and Christmas) so that they hang from the bars of the "T" shape. You might also assign several children to process in with candles that can be placed somewhere at the front of the church. If you use all of your aisles, you can involve several children in the procession without having it take too long.

The order of the procession should go as follows:

1. Anyone carrying banners or decorations.

2. Incense bearer (if incense is being used).

3. Cross bearer.

4. Altar servers.

5. Readers with the Book of the Gospels.

6. Priest celebrant.

Life Story   Everyday Praise

I am always telling people to use music in everyday classroom prayer so that children will begin to understand that it is a normal part of liturgy. My friend Vivian took that to heart, and began to use liturgical music in classroom prayer. They sang short pieces of hymns and, outside of Lent, always sang an "Alleluia" setting before reading from the Gospel. Groups of her eighth graders would take turns preparing and leading the prayer each day for a week. They usually wanted Vivian to lead the singing, though. Then, one day, a group of five boys who were scheduled to be the prayer leaders came to Vivian and said, "You don't have to lead the song. We know it and we'll start it." Vivian said that was fine. They turned away, but the one who was going to be the leader that day turned back and said, "Of course, you'll sing from the back of the room, won't you?" She said that she would. As it turned out, they did not need her help at all. Everyone in the class immediately picked up the song and sang out. From that point on, she rarely led the songs. One can only imagine what this experience of prayer in the classroom did for these young people's participation in Sunday Mass! Classroom prayer is an important part of teaching children about liturgical norms, reinforcing the role of the assembly, and encouraging confident ministers.

Step 6
Prepare Students for Their Roles

› # Getting Everyone Involved

As you begin to think about assigning roles to the children, remember that everyone already is involved in this liturgy, without needing to have a specific "part." Everyone in the group will participate in preparing the liturgy, talking about the readings, choosing music, writing the Prayer of the Faithful, and creating the liturgical environment.

As you consider how you will assign roles to the children, remember that you are planning a liturgy, not a school play. This is not a situation in which everyone who does not have a "part" gets left out. Everyone present at the Mass has an important role, whether they are sitting in the back pew or singing at the ambo. The goal is not to give everyone a specific ministerial role, but to create an environment in which the children understand their role as an assembly and grow in their relationship with God through active participation in the liturgy. Depending on the person and situation, serving in a ministerial role during the Mass can serve to distract from the liturgy, rather than deepening the experience of it. Think of the difference between attending a wedding as a guest and attending as a member of the wedding party. Sometimes, we become wrapped up in thinking about the additional responsibilities of our role and fail to notice what is going on around us. Don't let a desire to assign "parts" get in the way of allowing the children to have a deep experience of the liturgy.

That said, there are a variety of roles that children can perform before and during the liturgy that will help them to use their God-given abilities in service of the rest of the school or religious education community.

Pre-liturgy Roles

Liturgical Environment: If your group is responsible for planning and setting up some aspects of liturgical environment in the church, you might select a few children to take responsibility for this. These students can work with their classmates to craft any elements of environment that need to be made, and can take responsibility for placing them in the church ahead of time.

Worship Aid: If you are planning to make a worship aid, you might involve a few children in laying it out and decorating it.

Roles During the Liturgy

Assembly: We often forget it, but being a member of the assembly is a very important role. Prepare children to serve as members of the assembly by encouraging them to sing, speak the responses clearly, sit and stand up straight, remain quiet and attentive during the readings and homily, greet those nearby warmly during the sign of peace, maintain a reverent attitude during communion, and enjoy being together in the presence of God and all the saints! These are essential activities in the Mass.

Greeters: Greeters stand in the narthex or gathering area and greet everyone as they arrive. If you are handing out worship aids, greeters can distribute these, as well. Prepare children to be greeters by talking to them about times when they went to another person's house and felt welcomed. What did their host do to make them feel that way? Talk about how we can do similar things when greeting someone arriving at Mass. We can smile, greet them by name if we know their names, give them worship aids, and make sure that they know where to sit.

Altar Servers: Depending on the tradition in your school and the children's training and experience, some children in your group may be altar servers during the Mass. Only those who have gone through training should serve at the altar.

Music Ministers: If you have decided that children will be performing some of the music, make sure that you take time to prepare with them. Determine who can help them to prepare their parts, and identify some time when they can rehearse. Talk to them about what they might wear on the day of the liturgy.

Readers: If you have decided that children will be proclaiming the readings, prepare them by explaining that God speaks to us through the words of scripture, so it is important that we proclaim those words reverently and clearly. Practice the reading with them, and send home materials so they can practice with their families, too. Practice reading at least once in the church so that they know where they will need to stand. If you are using microphones, make sure that the microphones are on when you practice.

Processions: Make sure that you practice any processions with children ahead of time. If they will be carrying anything, like candles, incense, or banners, have those objects ready for them to practice with. Make sure that everyone knows the order in which they will walk. If some people in the procession, such as the altar servers or priest celebrant, are not available to practice processing with you, assign someone to stand in for them.

Bearers of Gifts: You might assign some children who will take the gifts forward when the time comes. Ahead of time, show the children where the gifts are and tell them when they should bring them forward. Practice doing this a few times. If you are working with very young children, you might assign someone to sit with them and let them know when they should bring the gifts up.

Life Story   Preparing to Sing

One year I was at a liturgy conference, helping my friend Kate prepare her teens to sing a song that one of the composers had written. One young woman had been asked to sing a solo. She had beauty, heart, and humility, but I could see that she had not yet developed the gift of fully diving into the text so that she could communicate its content and emotion. She was doing a very good job, but I knew that she could do better. First, I went to her and just sat with her for a moment. I joked around with her. Then, when I could see that she was not nervous anymore, I asked her to begin the song. Most people would probably never talk while someone else was singing, but I just kept shooting questions at her the entire time she was singing. Who was Jesus talking to here? How did that challenge make you feel? What is your tone when you share this story? Is your face expressing what your heart feels? How can you make me believe your commitment? The barrage continued until she was done. This probably created an out-of-body experience for this young girl, but I can tell you that she became an expressive, grace-filled young woman who continued her lifelong journey into the world of musical prayer. The lesson here is simple: young people are capable of great liturgy. They just need to be asked to rise to the occasion. When you accept watered-down liturgy for them, you fail to give them that opportunity. The goal is to create liturgy that they grow into, not out of.

Write the Prayer
of the Faithful

41

About the Prayer of the Faithful

The Prayer of the Faithful concludes the Liturgy of the Word and comes right before the Creed, or Profession of Faith. It is actually a set of prayers that follows a certain pattern—a pattern that teaches us to look beyond our own personal needs to those of the larger world. These prayers are sometimes called "intercessions" because through them, we fulfill our responsibility to intercede on behalf of the world.

In the intercessions, we pray for:

- The needs of the Church.
- Public authorities and the salvation of the whole world.
- Those burdened by any kind of difficulty.
- The local community.

The Parts of the Prayer of the Faithful

The Prayer of the Faithful should include:

Introductory Comment: This is something that the priest says before we pray the intercessions. The introductory comment is always addressed to the people, not to God or Jesus, since it is the priest's invitation to them to engage their priestly function of offering prayer. For example, the priest might say, "Jesus came to bring us salvation, and he has promised to come again. As we await his coming, let us pray."

Intercessions: The intercessions express the needs of the Church, world, oppressed, and local community. Usually, they follow the same basic format. We begin with the word "for," and end with the words, "we pray." We start out by naming the specific situation, and then expand upon it to make it more general. For example, you might say, "For all of the people in California whose homes were destroyed in the forest fires this week, and for all victims of natural disasters, we pray . . . " or "For Allison's grandmother and for all those who have died, we pray. . . . " At the end of the intercessions, we often pray for those who are sick and those who have died. It is best that you not lump together the names of the sick and the names of the dead into one intercession, as this can lead children to believe that those who are sick are going to die.

Assembly's Response: Often, we respond to intercessions by saying, "Lord, hear our prayer." This is a good response to use with children since it is widely used and easy to remember. Sometimes, writers of intercessions try to vary the acclamation. While permissible, this often results in confusion since the traditional response becomes an ingrained part of the ritual. Usually, it is best practice to go with whatever is ordinarily used in your parish.

Concluding Prayer: The Prayer of the Faithful concludes with a short prayer. Write this prayer using the "You, Who, Do, Through" formula:

1. YOU: Name God the Father (for example, "Loving Father, . . .").

2. WHO: Tell what God does. What is the quality of God you are appealing to? What did you hear in the scripture readings about God? (For example, "you sent us the gift of your Son.")

3. DO: Make this an action statement. What do you want God to do? In this case, we usually want him to hear our prayers. (For example: "Hear our prayers and grant them if it is your will.")

4. THROUGH: Conclude with the words, "We ask this through Christ our Lord. Amen."

If needed, remember to have your Prayer of the Faithful reviewed by the appropriate person or people in time to have it ready to go for the liturgy.

Writing the Prayer of the Faithful with Children

Involve the children in crafting the intercessions for the Prayer of the Faithful. Begin by reviewing your word chart once again. This will be your lexicon as you write the Prayer of the Faithful. You will be praying for the things that are going on in the world around you, but it is important that even the Prayers of the Faithful reflect the words that you hear in the readings. When the readings, the homily, the music, and the intercessions harmonize, it helps you to craft a liturgy that is experienced as a single breath.

Once you have reviewed the word chart, talk to the children about what is going on in the world today that needs our prayers. Write everyone's ideas on the board or on a sheet of newsprint. Go through the four things that we pray for—the Church, the world, the oppressed, and the local community—using the following questions as a guide. As you talk about the different things for which you might pray, continue to refer back to your word chart and use it as your source for words. For example, you might want to pray that the poor will experience the generous love of God. If the word *light* is on your word chart, you could phrase this desire by praying, "For the poor, that the Light of Christ will surround them and they will have what they need, we pray." This brief prayer encompasses both the need of the world and a theme of the readings.

Lead the children in writing the Prayer of the Faithful by asking the following questions:

1. The Church

• Remembering what we talked about, let's look at the word chart. Are there any words in there that we would use to pray for the Church?

• What things do you think the pope might be worried about right now? How should we pray for him?

2. The World

• What words on the word chart might people in the world need to hear today? Why?

• What big stories have you read about our president or the leaders of other nations in the news lately?

• What difficulties do you think our president or the leaders of other nations might be facing right now? How could God help in these situations?

3. The Oppressed

• Are there any words on the word chart that speak of suffering or oppression?

• When have you seen suffering of human beings? What happened?

• What have you seen in the news about people suffering this week?

• Are there any victims of natural disasters who might need our prayers?

• Are there any people suffering from injustice or violence who might need our prayers?

• Are there any people suffering from sickness or poverty who might need our prayers?

• How can God help in these situations?

4. The Local Community

• Are there any words on the word chart that you think are especially important for our community now?

• What needs have we seen in our parish, school, religious education program, neighborhood, or city? Is there anything "big" going on right now? How do we need God's help in these situations?

• Do you know any people who are sick?

• Do you know any people who have died recently?

You might also assemble Prayers of the Faithful, both for use in your school's liturgy and for use in regular classroom prayer, by placing a book for intentions on your prayer table or somewhere else in your space. Encourage the children to use this book to write the names of people, places, or situations for which they want to pray. Model an attitude of reverence for this book, and be sure that it is placed in a quiet area that doesn't see a lot of traffic. Encourage the children to be respectful of one another's space and need for quiet while they are writing their intentions. If you have a book of intentions, you may refer to the prayers within during your Prayer of the Faithful. You can simply say, "For all of the prayers in our book of intentions, and for all of the unspoken prayers in our hearts, we pray."

Step 8

Work with the Priest Celebrant

Why Meet with the Priest Celebrant?

Sometimes, for a variety of reasons, it might seem easier to just plan your parts of the liturgy and not involve the priest celebrant. It is important, though, that you do what you can to involve the priest celebrant in your preparation of the liturgy. For one thing, this gives you an opportunity to hear what the priest celebrant has planned to do and to ask any questions that you might have. It also gives you an opportunity to let the priest celebrant know what your class has been thinking about the readings. This might help the priest celebrant to plan his homily. Making sure that everyone is on the same page ahead of time will result in a more streamlined, meaningful liturgy for all those who participate.

Scheduling a Meeting

Ideally, you will be able to schedule a time for the priest celebrant to visit your class for about 30 minutes. About a week before you would like the priest celebrant to come to visit, issue an invitation. Try to offer a selection of at least three times when he might come to your classroom. You may want to check with your priest celebrant or his assistant ahead of time to find out any times of day that are exceptionally busy so that you can suggest times that are likely to fit in his schedule. Make sure that you provide him with a copy of the readings that you are using.

When scheduling time with the priest celebrant, keep in mind that priests are busy people with many competing responsibilities. Sometimes, there is just one priest who is charged with managing staff, performing liturgies, and providing pastoral care for an entire parish. That is a big job! Don't be offended if the priest celebrant winds up needing to reschedule as the time for your meeting approaches. Keep in mind that there are many unforeseen things that can spring up and demand a priest's attention, from broken furnaces to sick parishioners. Be flexible if something comes up, and try to schedule another time. Don't take a cancellation personally.

If your priest celebrant is unable to meet with you in person, tell him that you will be providing him with some notes from your class. Copy down the words from your word chart and give them to him, along with a brief note explaining what they are and how you came up with them. If any of the children said particularly insightful or surprising things while you were discussing the readings, provide a brief story of what happened. Let him know how he can reach you if he has any questions. If you did a video recording of your work with the children on the word chart, share it with the priest celebrant.

Preparing to Meet with the Priest Celebrant

Before meeting with the priest celebrant, prepare yourself and the children so that you are ready to speak with him. Tell the children that the priest is coming to hear about the preparation that they have done for the liturgy. Talk about any questions that the children might have for the priest celebrant about the liturgy or the readings, and write them down. Make sure that you have the word board ready to display. If you already have made music selections or written the Prayer of the Faithful, have those printed out and ready to show the priest celebrant.

Prepare the children by telling them what they may call the priest celebrant and how they should greet him. Think about how the priest likes to be addressed. Teach the children to say, for example, "Good morning, Father Smith," or "Hello, Father Jim."

Meeting with the Priest Celebrant

When the priest celebrant arrives, greet him and encourage the children to do the same. Show him where he may sit, and, very briefly, tell him what your class has done to prepare for the liturgy. Ask one or more of the students to read the words from the word board. Talk to him about your preparation, using the following questions as a guide:

When you look at our word board, what words stand most the most for you? Why?

What big things did you notice right away when you first read these readings?
(If the priest mentions any words that are not on your word board, consider adding them.)

Do you have any questions for us?
See if the priest has any questions for you. Allow the children to ask any questions that they might have. Be respectful of the priest's time and gracefully conclude your time together as scheduled. Have the children thank the priest.

Communication Tips When Working with the Priest Celebrant

- **Present information effectively.** Individuals are receptive to information in different ways. Some might be best contacted through e-mail, others on the phone. Some people need to read a written report ahead of time, where others prefer to hash it out in person. Find out how your priest celebrant likes to communicate and act accordingly.

- **Know who else to contact.** If your priest celebrant is unable to work with you, find out who else you might invite to your class. There might be a deacon or another member of the pastoral team who can meet with you and relay what is said back to the priest.

- **Be ready to change.** Remember: the priest celebrant has the last word in all matters related to the liturgy. If the priest wants to change something, you need to be ready to go with it. Talk about it to be sure that you understand the priest's reasoning and that he understands yours. This is an opportunity for you to learn about your priest celebrant's preferences.

- **Be flexible about timing.** It may take a few tries to schedule a time with your priest celebrant. Don't let that bother you, just keep doing your best to make it work. Understand that priests often have very full schedules.

- **Understand competing priorities.** Part of a priest's job is balancing the needs of all of the people in the parish. The priest may want to add or change something about your liturgy because of the needs of another group. Perhaps you can't put up banners because another group needs the church before your Mass, or maybe your school Mass is combined with the daily Mass in your parish, and the daily Mass crowd has different needs. Do your best to understand the situation and offer solutions.

- **Be prepared to "translate."** Many priests are wonderful at speaking to children, but in some cases priests might not be used to working with children, or may have accents that make it hard for children to understand them. If this is the case, help your priest celebrant to feel comfortable by making sure that the children understand what he is saying. You can do this by commenting on what he has said, for example: "I think it's really interesting that Father John saw images of light and of darkness in this psalm. What do you think about that?" Translate the children's responses back to him in the same way.

Step 9

Create the
Liturgical Environment

What is Liturgical Environment?

The word *liturgical environment* refers to all of the visual symbols that are used to enhance and support and experience of worship. We have liturgical environment in our churches. When you incorporate symbols and cloths in liturgical colors into the prayer space in your classroom, you are creating liturgical environment. When you set up an area where you can pray with your Advent wreath at home, that is liturgical environment, too.

Liturgical environment is not "decoration"; it is a very intentional arrangement of colors, images, and symbols that enhances the experience of worship. Think about some of the elements of liturgical environment that you have experienced. How does the shrouding of the crucifix in violet during Lent contribute to your experience of worship? How does it make you feel to come into the church on Easter Sunday and see white cloths and smell lilies? These colors and images bring the liturgy alive.

As you consider adding to the liturgical environment in your church, be very conscious of what you are doing and why. If there already are hanging banners present reflecting the liturgical colors, is it really going to enhance the space if you add additional banners reflecting something else? If you already have water in your space in the baptismal font, is there something you can do to focus attention on the presence of that water, without adding additional symbols of water? The environment should never hinder the liturgy. The environment should celebrate the tenor of the liturgy without distracting from it.

Steps for Planning Liturgical Environment

1. Assess what is already there. Usually, there already will be liturgical environment in place in your church. Before making any plans for environment, go to the church and see what is already there. Notice any banners or colors that you see. Take note of flowers, plants, or symbols. Be aware that liturgical environment often changes dramatically with the seasons, so if you are on the brink of seasonal change, you may want to check with someone to find out what will be coming next. Visiting the church during the last week of Ordinary Time, for example, won't give you a very good picture of how it will look during Advent.

2. Find out who is in charge of environment. In many parishes, there is someone (sometimes a volunteer) who is in charge of planning and setting up liturgical environment. If you don't know who this is, ask your parish liturgist or music minister.

3. Set a meeting with the person in charge of environment. Depending on schedules, this might just be a phone meeting. Or, if the person in charge of environment has time, you might invite him or her to visit your class. Talk to this person about what is already in place, and tell a little bit about the liturgy that you have planned. Perhaps this person might have some ideas about what you can do. Find out what this person is open to, and what is "off limits."

4. Decide what (if anything) you will do. Consider your word chart, the readings, and the liturgical time or season, and reflect on how that might be expressed through liturgical environment. If you like, you might have a conversation with the children to find out what they think. It could be that your parish church already has beautiful decorations in place. There may be no need to add anything.

5. Don't overdo it. Remember—liturgies with children should be minimal and essential, not overdone. If your parish already has beautiful decorations reflecting the symbols and colors of the liturgical time, there may be no need to add anything. Additional, competing colors or symbols often just serve to confuse and distract children.

◎ › Things to Avoid

- **Overwhelming the altar.** The whole liturgy points to the altar. The altar is the place where the most important part of the Mass—the transformation of bread and wine into the Body and Blood of Christ—occurs. For this reason, it is important that you are very careful about adding anything to the altar area. If you want to incorporate an idea into the liturgical environment, think of ways in which that idea can be expressed in the environment without placing anything extraneous on or before the altar.

- **Outdoing Sunday.** Remember, weekday liturgies prepare us for the Sunday liturgy. This won't work if the weekday celebration has a liturgical environment that outdoes, contradicts, or seems different from what you will see on Sunday.

- **Redundant or contradictory symbols.** Our churches already are rich with symbols, colors, and images. Adding elements to the liturgical environment sometimes can only serve to distract or confuse children, rather than contributing to their experience of worship. If there already are banners or draping in the liturgical colors in your church, for example, there's no need to add something else to enforce the liturgical colors—that element is already present. By the same token, it also is not particularly useful to add banners or draping expressing some other idea. That will only serve to confuse the children.

Thinking Outside the Box

- **Think beyond the altar.** Liturgical environment does not just mean what is up by the altar. You can provide environment in many other areas of your church. Consider what can be done to draw appropriate attention to the ambo. Bring environment into the aisles for opening and closing processions. Incorporate some environment in the narthex or welcoming space where you gather for Mass.

- **Moveable environment.** Often, the environment for the parish church is already set, which makes it difficult to incorporate anything additional. The environment team doesn't want to have to worry about moving or replacing anything that has already been put in place. In these instances, moveable elements of environment are a great way to add something without creating undue stress or difficulty. Banners, for example, can be carried in and out in the opening and closing procession. This way, there is no danger that you will forget and leave something behind that then has to be removed by someone else, and none of the existing environment needs to be disturbed.

Incorporating Local Traditions

As you think about liturgical environment, consider the diverse needs, backgrounds, and experiences of the families in your school or parish. What nationalities are represented among the children and their families? What kinds of things might the families be celebrating at home? Are there any major things going on in your town, parish, or school right now? Consider how these things can be incorporated into the environment as you gather to worship.

If you have many diverse cultures represented at your school, you might consider demonstrating that by setting up different areas in the environment of your gathering space that can reflect different cultural practices. During Christmas Time, for example, you might invite some families to bring in materials to set up a variety of nativity scenes that reflect different cultural traditions. During the month of May, traditionally dedicated to Mary, you might set up several Marian altars, each reflecting a different cultural celebration of Mary.

Another wonderful tradition is to set up an area with a book where children can write the names of those who have died during the month of November. Your parish may already do this, so check and find out. If they don't, obtain a book of the names of the dead (these are available from religious bookstores) and set it up in a special spot. You might consider surrounding it with some votive candles, or with small taper candles that can be stuck into a tray of sand. This can be set up somewhere in your church or gathering area. During the Prayer of the Faithful, you can refer to the names in the book when you pray for those who have died. ("For those whose names are listed in our book, and for all those who have died. . . .")

Life Story There Is a Way to Include Everyone

Once, when working in a Catholic school, I remember seeing one of the moms putting together some gifts that she had bought for the children in the second grade, who were about to receive the Sacrament of Penance for the first time. She had bought each of the children who would be receiving the sacrament a scapular and had written letters letting them know that all of the parents were proud of them and were praying for them as they received the sacrament. There were a few children in the second grade who were not Catholic. I saw that she had bought different small gifts for them and had written letters to them as well, letting them know that the parents loved them and were praying for them. I was gratified to see that she had thought of these children and had taken the time to let them know that, even though they were not baptized Catholics, they were loved and prayed for as part of our school community. I would imagine that small, loving gestures like this helped all of the kids, whether Catholic or not, to recognize and internalize the love that we are called to have for all of God's creation.

You need only think back to your own childhood to recognize the importance of inclusiveness. Allow your worship space to reflect the different cultures present in your school or parish. Invite non-Catholic children to participate in your prayer and worship by contributing intentions to your prayer book. Trust that this experience of the Church as community will stay with them as they grow older.

Step 10

Communicate with Other Faculty Members and the Catechetical Team

Your class may be preparing the liturgy, but there are probably many groups that will be participating in it. This is why it is important to communicate any important information to everyone who needs to know, in time for them to prepare for the liturgy. If you are doing anything out of the ordinary or if you require involvement of people outside of your class, it is imperative that you communicate this clearly. Nothing is worse than bringing your class to the liturgy and being totally surprised by something.

Prepare a Synopsis

Look at the entire liturgy, and prepare a one-page synopsis of what your class has prepared (look at the template at the end of the book for an example of how to do this). Note the readings and any songs that you have selected. If you are going to have anything out of the ordinary going on, such as movements during a song or a different kind of procession, make note of that. If you need any of the other teachers or catechists to do something, highlight that information. Make sure that this synopsis reaches not just the other teachers and catechists, but anyone else who needs to be "in the loop," like your principal, director of faith formation, or liturgist.

Make sure that you provide this communication early on. If you are going to need something from another teacher or class, request their help in person and secure their permission before issuing your synopsis. Do whatever you can to lower the pressure and let the rest of the teachers and catechists know what is going to be happening as soon as you can. Try to avoid asking the other teachers or catechists to do anything that is too hard or time consuming.

No Surprises!

Part of preparing liturgy is being aware of the community that will be experiencing the liturgy, and part of what forms us as community is ritual. Keep this in mind as you are planning what you will do. It can seem more fun or creative to deviate from what is ordinarily done, but consider how deviations from the norm will affect the rest of the community. People like feeling as if they are "at home" and know what they are doing when they come into church. No one likes feeling unsure of what they are supposed to do or where they are supposed to be. Those worries can distract from full participation in the liturgy. For this reason, it is very important to share any "new" elements of the liturgy with the rest of the teachers or catechists ahead of time so that they can prepare their classes for full participation.

› # Allow This to be a Teaching Moment

Your class has learned a lot from planning this liturgy. Consider sharing some of what you did with the other teachers or catechists. If there were some activities that went particularly well, for example, you might outline them in your synopsis so that other teachers can use them. If you will be using some new songs in the liturgy, consider arranging for your group to visit classes of younger children to teach them the songs.

Step 11
Rehearse

What Needs to be Rehearsed?

Any person who will have an active role in the liturgy, whether movement, music, or spoken word, needs to rehearse at least once before the day of the liturgy. You will need to rehearse the following roles:

- **Greeters:** Show greeters where they will stand. If they will be handing out worship aids, show them where the worship aids will be. Invite a few people to pretend to be arriving members of the assembly, and encourage the greeters to smile and say hello, give them a worship aid, and tell them where they may sit.

- **Altar Servers:** Usually altar servers will already be trained on how to perform their role, but be sure that any questions they may have are answered.

- **Music Ministers:** Any students who will be performing music should practice as an ensemble several times. If you will be using microphones, practice using them. Practice how students will come forth to perform music and return to their seats. Rehearse any cues so that the children know when to come forward. If students will be performing music that requires the assembly to sing, as well, invite them to practice looking out at the pews and smiling warmly so that the assembly will feel welcome to sing.

- **Readers:** Readers should practice proclaiming the reading from the ambo. If you will be using a microphone, practice with it. Show the readers how the Lectionary will be placed at the ambo, and have them practice going forward and returning to their seats. Rehearse any cues so that the children know when to come forward. You may want to have a few people sit in the pews as the readers practice so that the readers can practice making eye contact. These people can also indicate whether or not the readers can be heard.

- **Processions:** Practice opening and closing processions. Make sure that anyone carrying anything knows where it will be at the beginning and where it should be placed. Practice the procession with music so that you know how long it takes. If some members of the procession aren't there, such as the priest celebrant, assign someone to stand in that person's place.

- **Bearers of Gifts:** Make sure that bearers of gifts know where the gifts will be. Have them practice bringing them forward and returning to their seats. Practice with cues so that the children know when it is time for them to go forward.

What Needs to Happen at the Rehearsal?

Schedule at least 30 minutes for rehearsal. You will want to rehearse in the space where the liturgy will take place. If you are going to use microphones, make sure that they are on. If the children will be carrying anything, make sure that those objects are placed where they will be on the day of the liturgy. For example, you will want to make sure that empty dishes representing the gifts are placed where the gifts will be when the children go to bring them forward and that any banners or candles that will be brought up during the procession are placed wherever they will be when you gather to process on the day of the liturgy.

What If There Are Some Children Who Don't Have "Parts" to Rehearse?

Children who don't have any specific roles to rehearse can still be a very useful part of your rehearsal. Encourage them to spread out and be seated in the pews, so that all areas of the church are covered. When readers are practicing, the children can raise their hands to indicate whether or not they are able to hear. They also can check sight lines, making sure that no one is obscured by the ambo or liturgical environment. If you are using child musicians or cantors, have the children in the pews sing the assembly's parts and listen to be sure that the singers and instruments are balanced. Children without roles also can stand in for people who aren't there, such as taking the place of the priest celebrant in the opening and closing processions.

Life Story Don't Forget the Important Stuff!

When rehearsing with the children, it's important that you don't forget all of the preparation that you did together ahead of time. It is easy to let the work that you did discussing readings and selecting important words fall by the wayside and just make the rehearsal about logistics. Challenging children to be great ministers of liturgy can feel, at times, as though you are asking too much of them. The following story, contributed by one of my former students, Colleen, demonstrates that those challenging moments help children to grow, both in confidence and in faith.

Colleen tells the story of a time when she was nine years old and I asked her to perform one of the readings at the Easter Vigil. She and I met a few days before the Mass to go over the reading. She had thought that she would just stand at the ambo and read, but I wanted more from her. We began to talk about the waters of Baptism and renewal, and what those words really meant. I wanted her to use her voice and body to understand the reading and convey its meaning to the assembly. She grew nervous, and so I said, "Colleen, I know a lot of people and I know that if anyone can do this, you can." At the Vigil, she read beautifully. Afterward, people said to her, "How could you do that? You must have been so nervous, and you are so young." But she explained that she didn't do it alone—she was supported by our preparation together and guided by her own awareness of the presence of God. Colleen remembers this not as a time when she was anxious or confused, but as an important moment of encounter with God and growth in faith. Challenge the kids who you work with, and see how they respond!

Step 12

Review the Master Checklist

As the time of the liturgy approaches, you probably have been making lots of little notes to yourself about things that you need to do.

This checklist will help you to make sure that everything is done before the big day. There's space for you to add things to it, too.

 # The Master Checklist

Prepare:

Make sure that the following has been prepared in advance of the liturgy.

❑ Readings have been selected and readers have been chosen. Readings have been sent home with child readers so that they can prepare.

❑ Music has been selected and music leaders have been identified.

❑ Prayers of the Faithful have been written and readers have been chosen.

❑ Liturgical environment has been discussed and prepared.

❑ Worship aids, if needed, have been prepared.

❑ Opening and closing processions have been planned.

❑ Ministers have been chosen (greeters, readers, bearers of gifts, musicians, altar servers, those participating in processions).

❑ Will you have a sacristan? If so, provide him or her with a step-by-step description of your liturgy so that he or she knows what to do. If not, figure out who will prepare your space for the liturgy (there is more information about this in Step 13).

_____

_____

_____

_____

_____

_____

_____

Have:

Make sure that you have the following items finished and ready to go.

❏ Any items for opening and closing processions, such as banners or candles, finished and on hand.

❏ Prayers of the Faithful updated, printed, and placed in binder.

❏ Worship aids printed and ready to hand out.

❏ Liturgical environment completed and ready to place.

_____

_____

_____

_____

_____

Contact:

Contact the following people. Make sure that they are coming and know the date, time, and place.

❏ Priest celebrant.

❏ Principal or director of religious education.

❏ Other teachers or catechists.

❏ Adult volunteers.

❏ Adult musicians.

❏ Parents of everyone in the class.

_____

_____

_____

_____

_____

Don't Forget!

Sometimes, the simplest things wind up being overlooked. As you are preparing for the liturgy, consider the following often-forgotten questions:

Who will make sure that the lights are turned on and the doors are unlocked?

If you are using microphones, who will make sure that they are in place and turned on? Will anyone be around to troubleshoot if the microphones aren't working properly?

Does the priest celebrant have everything that he needs?

If the priest celebrant normally celebrates Mass at another location, will he be bringing his own Missal or is he expecting you to have one?

Have you reviewed the Prayers of the Faithful in light of recent events? Has anything happened in the days since you wrote the Prayers of the Faithful, like a death in your community or devastating natural disaster in another part of the world, that you should incorporate into the intentions?

Will people who don't usually attend liturgies with you, such as parents or grandparents, be attending this liturgy? What signage or direction will they need to find parking, restrooms, and the space where you will be celebrating the liturgy?

What is happening after the liturgy? If you are planning a reception, for example, make sure that you consider everything needed for the reception in your checklist for the liturgy. How will you move everyone from the liturgy to the reception?

Consider Finding a "Stage Manager"

You have been working hard to get everything ready for the liturgy. On the day of the liturgy, consider taking a step back and assigning someone else the job of "stage manager," making sure that everyone is in the right place at the right time. Perhaps a parent volunteer or an older student can serve in this role. Instead of running around to get everything ready yourself, take the role of "producer." You have done a lot to bring this about, and now your job is to experience it. Join the children with whom you have prepared the liturgy and pray with them. Mass is an equalizing experience. Barriers of age and authority are stripped from you and the children before God. You pray together as equals. Fully engaging in prayer alongside the children who have participated in the preparation of the liturgy enables you to share their experience, which will make engaging them in mystagogical reflection (which you will see in Step 15), a much more fruitful experience.

› Make Your Backup Plan

In the days leading up to the liturgy (and even on the day of the liturgy itself), things may go wrong. Children may forget what you taught them about their ministerial roles, for example, or adults who you had asked to volunteer might cancel on you. When this happens, don't let it put too much pressure on you. Remain calm. Look at the checklist again, and remind yourself that you did a good job preparing for this week. Then, make your backup plan, considering the following questions:

Is this something that you really need for the liturgy, or can you do without it?

If you can do without it, then don't worry about it. If the banners for the procession don't get done, process in without banners. If the gift bearer who was supposed to carry the wine calls in sick, have the child who was going to carry up the water carry up the wine as well.

Who else can fill this role?

In case a minister calls in sick or doesn't show up, consider who else might fill their role. The librarian is a great person to ask to be a reader. Perhaps there are some parents or teachers / catechists who can substitute as musicians if need be.

Who can help out?

If there is an emergency that can't be solved easily, ask for help. Know which parents might be available and willing to pitch in. Talk to the other teachers or catechists and see if they have any ideas.

Step 13

It's the Day of the Liturgy

◎> Getting the Church Ready

Before the liturgy begins, someone needs to ready the church. If you have a sacristan at your disposal, make sure that you communicate with that person ahead of time so that he or she knows what you have planned. If you are doing anything outside of the norm, make sure that the sacristan understands what you are doing. Keep the lines of communication between you and the sacristan open. A simple, "Are we okay? Is there anything else you need from me?" can help to keep things calm and reduce unnecessary confusion.

If you do not have a sacristan at your disposal, then you will need to work with the liturgist, musician, priest, or whomever else might be "in charge" to get the church ready for the Mass. You or an appointee will need to do the following:

- Prepare the gifts and place them on the table or in the place from which they will be brought forward during the Liturgy of the Eucharist.

- Prepare the Missal with the proper ribbons (you will want to communicate with the liturgist or priest celebrant to make sure that this is done properly).

- Set the Lectionary out with the page open to the correct readings for the day.

- Make sure that the Prayers of the Faithful are in a binder and placed in the appropriate location.

- Make sure that the microphone heights are right. Test the microphones to see if they are working.

- Make sure that the music area is set up. If chairs, stands, sheet music, or instruments are needed, make sure that they are in place. Test and place any microphones.

- If you are using worship aids, make sure that they are where they need to be.

◎> Getting the Ministers Ready

You may want to ask those who will serve as ministers to show up early so that you can do a head count and have enough time to seek suitable replacements for anyone who is not present. Then, make sure that your ministers are prepared by doing the following:

- Show greeters where to stand and make sure that they are in place. Show them where the worship aids are, if you are using worship aids.

- Get those participating in the opening procession into line in a space where they may wait until the time comes. If they will be carrying anything in, make sure that they have those items.

- Tell readers that the Lectionary has been opened to the appropriate readings and show them where it is. Allow them to go up to the ambo to practice saying a line or two, if time allows. Show the readers where to sit in a spot near the ambo. If readers will be doing readings with partners, make sure that they are seated together.

- Gather musicians in the music area and make sure that they have what they need. If any musicians need to tune or warm up, show them where they may do that.

- If you are using extraordinary ministers of holy communion, make sure that they know where they are going to be standing if they are not familiar with your space. Use only those ministers who have been through training.

- Show gift bearers where the gifts are, and show them where they may sit in a spot near the gifts.

- Show readers of the Prayers of the Faithful where the binder containing the prayers is. If you have added or revised some petitions in light of recent events, tell them. Show them where they may sit, in a spot near the front of the church.

Getting the Assembly Ready

Before the liturgy, make sure that you prepare the children who will be part of the assembly, too. This will be much easier for you to do if you have assigned a "stage manager" to take care of preparing the church and the ministers. If you need to do these things yourself, then assign someone else, such as a teacher's aide, parent volunteer, or a few older students, to gather the children in your group and help them enter into the space for the liturgy and find their seats.

If the children are going to the liturgy first thing upon arrival at school or religious education, then you will want to tell them ahead of time where they can find you so that you can sit together as a group. Perhaps you can identify a spot in the gathering area where you all will meet. If you are unable to meet them, tell them who will be gathering with them so that they know who to look for. Enter into the space for the liturgy together, and sit as a group. If possible, assign a parent or an aide to wait outside for any latecomers and help them to join you where you are seated.

If you are having the liturgy in the middle or at the end of your other school or religious education activities, take time to prepare your group for what they are about to experience. Perhaps you might talk a little bit about some of the things that they are excited to see or hear, or some of the words or songs that will hold special meaning for them today. Maybe some of the children have special things that they would like to pray for at the Mass.

You will also want to prepare the children to be still for a while. Be sure to take time for a bathroom break before going to the space for the liturgy. Make sure that children leave behind any toys or objects that might prove distracting. If the liturgy is the first thing happening in the day and the children are entering with books or backpacks, consider another place where you might keep these during the liturgy so that they don't prove to be distractions. If you are working with very young children, you may want to engage in some simple physical activity in the time before the liturgy, like a few rounds of "Head, Shoulders, Knees, and Toes" or a game of "The Good Shepherd Says" (played to the same rules as "Simon Says") to make it easier for them to be still for a while.

It is best if you can sit and pray with your class during the Mass. You all worked together on this liturgy, and you should experience it as a group. You and the children have come to the table as equals, with a desire to praise and honor Jesus Christ.

Before leaving for the space where the liturgy will be held, take a moment in prayer. Call God's Spirit down upon all of you who have prepared the liturgy, and all of the people who will be members of the congregation. You may use the prayer below, or another prayer that you like.

 ## Prayer before the Mass

God of love and light,
you call us to walk with you every day of our lives.
Bless the work we do as we share the Word of God.
Let us learn ways of peace and understanding
        from your Son, Jesus.
Send your Spirit to inspire our hearts and minds.
We ask this through Christ our Lord.
Amen.

Step 14

Be Prepared to Handle Any Situation during the Liturgy

As you are experiencing the liturgy, remember that liturgy is prayer.

You have worked hard to plan this liturgy, and you may feel a need to rush around and make sure that everything is going "right." But liturgy is real and alive. It is the work of human hands. Therefore, mistakes will be made. When things go wrong, just focus on restoring the prayer experience. It's okay if you get off script, so long as the experience of prayer goes on. If something goes wrong, lower the stakes. Remain calm, and have a backup plan.

The Top Five Most Common Things That Go Wrong (And How to Solve Them)

1. A child minister called in sick. If a child calls in sick, first consider whether you really need someone to serve in this role. Can you get through the songs with four singers instead of five? Is it okay to have one fewer greeter? Often, you can do with one less. If the child is in a vital role, such as a reader for example, then consider who else can serve in the role. The school librarian is a great choice for a reader. Other teachers or catechists and older children also can step up and take on ministerial roles.

2. The musician won't be there. If the musician cannot make it in, consider your other options. Are there other teachers or catechists who might be able to provide accompaniment for some of the songs? If you have people who can play the piano but who do not feel strong enough to sight-read, find out what other songs they do know. Perhaps you can swap out some of the music. If you cannot find anyone to provide accompaniment, you may have to go *a cappella*. If this is the case, you may want to consider your music selections. If you picked some songs that your community hasn't sung often, it may be hard for them to sing them without accompaniment. You may have an easier time singing familiar hymns.

3. The priest celebrant couldn't be there, so another priest is coming in who doesn't know anything about what you've done. If this happens, be flexible. Remember that the priest celebrant has the final word in any matters related to the liturgy. If this new priest celebrant wants you to change something about the liturgy, just do your best to accommodate his request. Be assured that most priests who substitute will try to accommodate the group they are serving.

4. Elements of liturgical environment didn't get done. If this happens, just let it go. There is nothing needed beyond the simplest elements of environment. There is no sense in rushing around on the day of the liturgy trying to get things finished.

5. The ministers are forgetting what they were taught to do. Especially if you are using young children as ministers, you may have a few hiccups during the Mass. Perhaps a child goes forward to read but then cannot find the reading on the page, or the time comes for the gifts to be brought forth, but the gift bearers aren't sure whether they are supposed to go yet. If this happens, try to avoid calling out or gesticulating, as this can be distracting and can cause others to feel anxiety. Don't let little mistakes turn into a big deal. Simply rise and, slowly and prayerfully, go to the child who is confused and wordlessly guide him or her to the spot where he or she needs to be. If a child reader cannot find his or her spot, go up to the ambo, point to the place on the page, and stand beside the child as he or she reads. When the child is finished, walk back to your seats together. If a child gift bearer does not go forth at the appropriate time, walk back to the place where the gifts are kept, make eye contact and smile at the gift bearer, and walk forward with the gifts together. Allow everything, even mistakes, to be part of a seamless experience of prayer.

The Importance of Ritual

It may not seem like it, but ritual is a key part of ensuring that few things go wrong during the liturgy. When planning liturgies, focus on simplifying them so that the children can truly take the ritual of Mass into their hearts. Make sure that what the children experience in your liturgies together leads them to what they experience at Mass with their families on Sunday. Follow the local customs and traditions of the parish where the children attend Mass. If your parish sings the "Our Father," for example, follow suit in your liturgy. If your parish commonly uses certain hymns during Lent or during communion, use those same hymns.

If you adhere to ritual and resist the urge to break away or do something unusual, then the child's participation in the liturgy becomes as natural and effortless as breathing. The children know where to go and what to do without even thinking about it because they have seen it done so many times. If something goes wrong, the children instinctively know how to correct it on their own because the liturgy is an ingrained part of their beings.

Compare the ritual of your liturgies to the other rituals that we celebrate in our lives, like the ritual of a birthday. When it comes time to celebrate a birthday in your household, you probably don't have to spend much time agonizing over the right thing to do. You already know what song you will sing and what kinds of special foods or activities you might plan. If it comes to be time to light the candles on the cake and you can't find matches, it doesn't turn into a party-ruining panic. You don't need to assign someone ahead of time to lead you in singing "Happy Birthday." Throughout, you unconsciously improvise and do everything in the spirit of the celebration. Because you know the ritual, you know what to do in times when things go wrong. The same can be true of the ritual of the Mass.

Life Story Trained by Ritual

Once I was invited to prepare the liturgical dancers from my parish to serve in an important liturgy at a conference, where our cardinal would be the presider. I had rehearsed them ahead of time, thinking everything was fine. We were in the middle of the liturgy, just before the preparation of the gifts, and I realized that I had completely forgotten to choreograph anything for this part of the Mass. The altar was going to be set as part of the preparation of the gifts, and I had done nothing to plan for it. I was sitting there with my head down as the song was starting, thinking, "I hope someone tells them what to do." And all of a sudden there was this popping sound. I looked to the right of the altar area, and there were my dancers, taking a white cloth, pulling it taut, and carrying it forth in the procession. They walked to the altar and they set it reverently, even though they were in an unfamiliar, high-stakes environment and nothing had been done to prepare them. I realized that they knew what to do because we had repeated this same thing every time the dancers were at the Mass at our parish at home. Even though nothing had been planned or said to them, they knew what to do because they had done it so many times before. It was an incredible moment. And that's when I realized that spontaneity could only happen because it was a ritual that they knew inside out.

Step 15

Mystagogy: What Happened and What Did You Learn?

The liturgy is over, but wait—you are not finished yet!

After the liturgy, it is important that you engage in *mystagogy* (MISS-tuh-go-gee), a process of unpacking everything that you experienced and learning from it. Mystagogy is important because it gives you the opportunity to remember, dialogue about, and celebrate what you just saw.

Mystagogy is a big word, but, believe it or not, it can all be summed up in three basic questions: What happened? What does it mean to me? How will it change my life? Whether we realize it or not, we perform mystagogy all the time. Just watch any episode of the old TV show "Doogie Howser" and watch the segment at the end when Doogie (a 16-year-old prodigy who works as a doctor) writes in his journal on his computer. You will notice that he often reflects on his experience using the same formula: What happened? *I moved out of my parents' house.* What does it mean to me? *I'm scared.* How will it change my life? *I'm alone.* This is mystagogy, in its simplest form.

Use these three questions with the children in order to perform mystagogy after the liturgy.

1. What happened?

Begin by asking the students what they remember about the liturgy they just celebrated. Be ready to write down everything that they say on the board or on a sheet of chart paper. Begin by prompting the children with some questions, going through the Mass chronologically. Does anyone remember anything about the entrance procession? Does anyone remember anything about how the priest greeted you? If there are no answers, sit in the silence. After some time, continue to prompt. Does anyone remember what song we sang when we walked in? Were there any words in that song that were interesting? Make sure that you allow plenty of time for the children to think, so that every child has the chance to vocalize what is in his or her heart.

2. What did it mean to me?

Once you have a list of some of the important things that happened, unpack the mystery by asking more questions. You might call upon a child who mentioned a certain song and say, "You said that song was really great. Why did you think so? Was it the beat? The words? Or did the whole song just make you want to do something better for the Church?" Record the things that the children say. Remember that there is no right or wrong in this time. This is an unpacking of the child's experience. Focus on listening to and affirming what the children experienced and felt, rather than taking over the conversation with "teaching."

3. How will it change my life?

Even very young children can have life-changing experiences as a result of the liturgy. Perhaps you might make a list of "action words" that spring forth from what the children have said. For example, if a child heard that Jesus wants us to love others as God loves us, then you might simply rephrase that and write, "I will love others as God loves me." Engage the children in thinking of ways in which that action might be taken in their own lives. For example, loving others as God loves us would mean not pushing to be first in line, and sharing belongings.

Outline of the Mass

Introductory Rites

The Introductory Rites "ensure that the faithful, who come together as one, establish communion and dispose themselves properly to listen to the Word of God and to celebrate the Eucharist worthily" (GIRM, 46).

Action	Purpose/Description (paraphrases / quotations from the *General Instruction of the Roman Missal*)	Always, Optional, Customary	Your Class's Role
Entrance Song and Procession	Foster unity and introduce the liturgical time or season.	Always.	Your class may be responsible for selecting music and participating in the procession.
Rite of Blessing and Sprinkling with Holy Water	"From time to time . . . instead of the customary Penitential Act, the blessing and sprinkling of water may take place as a reminder of Baptism" (GIRM, 51).	Optional—often done on Sundays during Easter Time.	
Penitential Act (including Kyrie Eleison)	We are invited to recall our sins in order to prepare us to celebrate worthily. This is not the same thing as the Sacrament of Penance: the priest does not say "I absolve you," but rather asks that God will forgive us.	Always.	
Gloria	An ancient hymn that glorifies and entreats God.	On Sundays outside the seasons of Advent and Lent; on solemnities and feasts.	
Collect (KAHL-ukt)	Gathers (or "collects") the prayers of the people and expresses the character of the celebration	Always.	

Liturgy of the Word

". . . in the readings, as explained by the Homily, God speaks to his people . . . and Christ himself is present through his word in the midst of the faithful" (GIRM, 55).

First Reading	Usually from the Old Testament, New Testament letters, or Acts of the Apostles.	Always at regular Masses. In Masses with children, the First Reading may be omitted so long as the Gospel is proclaimed.	Students who have received adequate training may be invited to proclaim the First Reading.
Responsorial Psalm	Like the other readings, this is the Word of God. It expresses a wide range of human emotions and fosters meditation on the entire Word of God.	Best practice is to sing the psalm. In any case, the psalm normally should be sung or proclaimed from the ambo, as with the other readings.	Your class may be responsible for selecting the setting of the psalm. If there are trained cantors among the students, they may be invited to sing.
Second Reading	From Letters of the New Testament.	Only on Sundays, solemnities, and feasts. In Masses with children, the Second Reading may be omitted so long as the Gospel is proclaimed.	Students who have received adequate training may be invited to proclaim the Second Reading.
Gospel Acclamation	Sung as we stand to hear the Gospel, it expresses great reverence for the Gospel.	Always. Outside of Lent the acclamation is "Alleluia."	

Action	Purpose/Description (paraphrases / quotations from the General Instruction of the Roman Missal)	Always, Optional, Customary	Your Class's Role
Gospel	Always from one of the four accounts of the Gospel: Matthew, Mark, Luke, or John.	Always.	
Homily	The homily relates the readings to "both the mystery being celebrated and the particular needs of the listeners" (GIRM, 65).	Highly recommended.	
Profession of Faith	The people respond to all that they have heard in the readings and homily and confess the great mystery of faith.	Always on Sundays and solemnities.	
Prayer of the Faithful	For the needs of the entire Church and the salvation of the whole world.	Always.	Your class may prepare and proclaim.

Liturgy of the Eucharist

"At the Last Supper Christ instituted the Paschal Sacrifice and banquet, by which the Sacrifice of the Lord is continuously made present in the Church, whenever the priest, representing Christ the Lord, carries out what the Lord himself did and handed over to his disciples to be done in his memory" (GIRM, 35).

Action	Purpose/Description	Always, Optional, Customary	Your Class's Role
Preparation of the Gifts	The gifts, which will become Christ's Body and Blood, are brought forward by the faithful.	Always. Customary to accompany with a song.	Students may bring the gifts forward; class may choose song.
Prayer over the Offerings	The priest prays over the gifts. "The people, joining in this petition, make the prayer their own by means of the acclamation *Amen*" (GIRM, 77).	Always.	
Eucharistic Prayer	". . . the center and high point of the entire celebration . . . the prayer of thanksgiving and sanctification" (GIRM, 78).	Always.	
Acclamation: Holy, Holy, Holy	The congregation joins with the heavenly powers to sing the Holy, Holy, Holy.	Always. Best practice to sing, using one of the parish Mass settings.	
Epiclesis (ep-uh-KLEE-suhs)	". . . the Church implores the power of the Holy spirit that the gifts . . . be conscrated, . . . for the salvation of those who will partake of it" (GIRM, 79).	Always.	
Institution narrative and Consecration	The Church recounts the institution of the Eucharist at the Last Supper.	Always.	
Anamnesis (an-uhm-NEE-suhs); Memorial Acclamation	". . . the Church . . . celebrates the memorial of Christ, recalling especially his blessed Passion, glorious Resurrection, and Ascension" (GIRM, 79).	Always. Best practice to sing, using same parish Mass setting as Holy Holy Holy.	
Oblation	The Church offers the sacrificed Christ and all offer themselves.	Always.	
Intercessions	The Eucharist is celebrated in communion with the entire Church, heavenly and earthly, for all her members, living and dead.	Always.	

Action	Purpose/Description (paraphrases / quotations from the General Instruction of the Roman Missal)	Always, Optional, Customary	Your Class's Role
Final doxology / Amen	Praise and glorification of God is confirmed by the people's Amen.	Always. Best practice is to sing, using same parish Mass setting as the two earlier acclamations.	
Communion Rite:	". . . in keeping with the Lord's command, his Body and Blood should be received" as spiritual food by the faithful who are properly disposed (GIRM, 80).	Always.	
Lord's Prayer	Community prays for "daily bread" and forgiveness before receiving.	Always.	
Rite of Peace	". . . the Church entreats peace and unity for herself and for the whole human family" (GIRM, 82).	Always.	
The Fraction of the Bread and the Lamb of God	Breaking of bread signifying that the many receive from the one Bread of Life that is Christ.	Always. Best practice is to sing, using a parish Mass setting.	
Communion	The faithful process to receive while singing a unifying song.	Always.	Your class may choose the song.
Prayer after Communion	The priest brings the prayer of the People of God to completion and prays for the fruits of the mystery just celebrated (GIRM, 89).	Always.	

Concluding Rites

The people are sent forth "so that each may go back to doing good works, praising and blessing God" (GIRM, 90).

Action	Purpose/Description	Always, Optional, Customary	Your Class's Role
Announcements	The priest or another reader announces anything that the assembled community needs to know.	Customary.	Your class may write the announcements. Students who have been prepared may read the announcements.
Blessing	The priest prays over the people.	Always.	
Dismissal	The people are sent forth to do good works and honor God with their lives.	Always.	
Closing song	A song is sung as the priest and ministers process out.	Customary.	Your class may choose the closing song and students may participate in the procession.

Worksheet for Writing The Prayer of the Faithful

Response:

_____

_____

_____

Introductory Comment:

_____

_____

_____

Intercessions:

For the Church:

For_____, that _____

_____

_____, we pray:

For the World:

For_____, that _____

_____

_____, we pray:

For the Oppressed:

For_____, that _____

_____

_____, we pray:

For the Local Community:

For_____, that _____

_____

_____, we pray:

Concluding Prayer:

_____(YOU)

_____(WHO)

_____(DO)

We ask this through Christ our Lord. Amen.

Synopsis to Provide to Other Teachers or Catechists

Hi!

_____ (class) is preparing the Mass for _____ (date) and we wanted

to help you to prepare for the liturgy. We have been doing a lot of work to prepare for the Mass.

The readings for the Mass will be:

(Write the reading citations.) _____

_____

_____

We have read these readings and have noticed some words that stand out to us, including:

(Provide some words from your word board.) _____

_____

_____

We will also hear some of these words in the hymns that we will be singing, including:

(Provide some song names.) _____

_____

_____

You can help us to prepare for the Mass by:

(Write any special instructions.) _____

_____

_____

Thank you for helping us to prepare for the Mass that we will celebrate together. If you have

any questions, please contact:

(Teacher or catechist's name:) _____

_____

_____

Note Home to Parents of Readers

Hello,

Your child _____ (name) has been chosen as a reader for the liturgy that will

take place on _____ (date) at _____ (time). Please

help to prepare your child at home by reading through the attached scripture together. Invite

your child to proclaim the reading to you and the other members of your family and encourage

your child to make eye contact and to speak loudly and clearly. If there are some words that

your child does not know how to pronounce, look them up together.

Rehearsal for the liturgy will take place on _____ (date) at _____ (time)

at _____ (place). If you would like to watch your child proclaim the

readings, please join us at the rehearsal or the liturgy. If you want to photograph or film your

child reading, please understand that this will be allowed only at the rehearsal.

Thank you for your role in assisting your child's preparation.

_____ (signature)

☑ The Master Checklist

Prepare:

Make sure that the following has been prepared in advance of the liturgy.

❑ 1. Readings have been selected and readers have been chosen. Readings have been sent home with child readers so that they can prepare.

❑ 2. Music has been selected and music leaders have been identified.

❑ 3. Prayers of the Faithful have been written and readers have been chosen.

❑ 4. Liturgical environment has been discussed and prepared.

❑ 5. Worship aids, if needed, have been prepared.

❑ 6. Opening and closing processions have been planned.

❑ 7. Ministers have been chosen (greeters, readers, bearers of gifts, musicians, altar servers, those participating in processions).

❑ 8. Will you have a sacristan? If so, provide him or her with a step-by-step description of your liturgy so that he or she knows what to do. If not, figure out who will prepare your space for the liturgy. (There is more information in Step 13).

Have:

Make sure that you have the following items finished and ready to go.

❑ 1. Any items for opening and closing processions, such as banners or candles, finished and on hand.

❑ 2. Prayers of the Faithful updated, printed, and placed in binder.

❑ 3. Worship aids printed and ready to hand out.

❑ 4. Liturgical environment completed and ready to place.

Contact:

Contact the following people. Make sure that they are coming and know the date, time, and place.

❑ 1. Priest celebrant.

❑ 2. Principal or director of religious education.

❑ 3. Other teachers or catechists.

❑ 4. Adult volunteers.

❑ 5. Adult musicians.

❑ 6. Parents of everyone in the class.

Prayer before the Mass

God of love and light,
you call us to walk with you every day of our lives.
Bless the work we do as we share the Word of God.
Let us learn ways of peace and understanding
        from your Son, Jesus.
Send your Spirit to inspire our hearts and minds.
We ask this through Christ our Lord.
Amen.